To Chuck Hutton

With heartfelt thanks for
your friendship and your
excellent and willing help.

Dave Myers
9/19/80

THE INFLATED SELF

THE
INFLATED
SELF

Human Illusions and the
Biblical Call to Hope

DAVID G. MYERS

The Seabury Press · New York

1980
The Seabury Press
815 Second Avenue
New York, N.Y. 10017

Printed in the United States of America

Library of Congress Cataloging in Publication Data
Myers, David G   The inflated self.
Includes bibliographical references and index.
1. Good and evil. 2. Belief and doubt. 3. Hope.
I. Title.
BJ1401.M86   241'.3   80-16427   ISBN 0-8164-0459-3

Grateful acknowledgment is made to the following publishers for permission to use the materials listed:

American Psychological Association for a chart excerpted from "Meta-
Analysis of Psychotherapy Outcome Studies," by Mary Lee Smith
and Gene V. Glass which appeared in volume 32 of the *American
Psychologist*.

Faber and Faber Ltd for excerpts from "The Love Song of J. Alfred
Prufrock" and "The Hollow Men" in *Collected Poems 1909–1962*
by T. S. Eliot.

Harcourt Brace Jovanovich, Inc. for excerpts from "The Love Song of
J. Alfred Prufrock" in *Collected Poems 1909–1962* by T. S. Eliot, and
for excerpts from the "The Hollow Men" in *Collected Poems 1909–
1962* by T. S. Eliot, copyright 1936 by Harcourt Brace Jovanovich,
Inc.; copyright 1963, 1964 by T. S. Eliot.

Three Rivers Poetry Journal for the poem "The Healers" by Jack Ridl.

To my parents
Kenneth Gordon Myers
Luella Nelson Myers

Lord, I have given up my pride
    and turned away from my arrogance.
I am not concerned with great matters
    or with subjects too difficult for me.
Instead, I am content and at peace.
As a child lies quietly in its mother's arms,
    so my heart is quiet within me.
Israel, trust in the Lord
    now and forever!

Psalm 131

Contents

Acknowledgments

It is great folly to seek to
be wise . . . on one's own.
LA ROCHEFOUCAULD

It is my good fortune to be part of a Christian intellectual community that includes many people who are both competent scholars and self-giving individuals. Hundreds of sensitive suggestions by my friend Jack Ridl, poet and writer, significantly improved this book's clarity and readability. Robert Coughenour, Charles Huttar, Thomas Ludwig, Donald Luidens, Carol Myers, and Merold Westphal each read most or all of the manuscript and offered suggestions that resulted in dozens of changes. Other persons—Sharon Carnahan, Jane Dickie, Paul Fries, Lars Granberg, Eugene Heideman, Steven Hoogerwerf, Kevin Kennedy, Sang Lee, Kim Osterman, Gerard Van Heest, David Paap, Robert Palma, Barrie Richardson, John Shaughnessy, Richard Thayer, Margaret Van Wylen, Allen Verhey, and Dennis Voskuil —read portions in which they had special interest or expertise and shared countless observations concerning both the writing and the ideas. Additional hours of conversation spent with many of these friends have enriched and stimulated me. To each one of them, I owe a debt of gratitude.

Special thanks are also due the Lilly Endowment, for its financial support, and Fuller Theological Seminary, where an earlier version of this book was presented as the 1979 Finch

Lectures. It was an extra pleasure to have the week at Fuller planned and coordinated by one of my former students, Hendrika Vande Kemp. Finally, I am indebted to my friends Phyllis Vandervelde, Karen Alderink, and Maxine Mesbergen for their predictably excellent typing services.

Introduction

From the story of the fall through the parable of the prodigal son, the Bible portrays the drama of our sin and self-deceit. This drama is central to the biblical understanding of the human condition. "It might even be said," concluded S. J. De Vries in the *Interpreter's Dictionary of the Bible*,

> that in the Bible man has only two theological concerns involving himself: his sin and his salvation. Man finds himself in sin and suffers its painful effects; God graciously offers salvation from it. This, in essence, is what the Bible is about.[1]

If this biblical understanding of human sin is living truth, not just speculation, then it will have observable consequences. Confirmation of these presumed consequences may make sin more intelligible, thus strengthening the credibility of biblical faith in the modern age. As Augustine noted, faith should always seek understanding. It is for that end that this book attempts to converge the modern research perspective with the ancient biblical perspective on our human condition.

Part I, "The Dynamics of Evil," develops the scientific complement to recent social essays on the reality of sin (notably, Karl Menninger's *Whatever Became of Sin?* and Henry Fairlie's *The Seven Deadly Sins Today*). Research psychologists have not said much about evil. In *Psychological Abstracts* the word evil is not an index term and, of the nearly 300,000 titles cited between 1967 and 1978, it appears in only seventeen. However, some behavioral science insights regarding evil do exist, and are waiting to be assembled into a psychology of human evil. New scientific testimonies to humanity's selfishness and greed parallel the biblical account of the inner sources of human evil. Laboratory demonstrations of the corrupting effects of evil situations and of evildoing remind us that evil power can seduce even well-meaning individuals. Most striking of all is the mass of new evidence documenting the extent of human pride, both personal and collective. Perhaps this new version of an old story can drive home its truth.

Part II, "Illusions of Human Thought," views the biblical theme of human finiteness from the perspective of recent laboratory experiments. New research on the foibles and fallacies of human thought is rolling off the presses faster than anyone can peruse it. These experiments give fresh insight into why people believe things that are not true. To us proud individuals in a self-righteous culture, it is shocking to discover that one of the brute facts of human nature is our capacity for illusion and self-deception. We shall see how false beliefs are formed and how these thought distortions operate 1) to create belief in ESP, and 2) an inflated confidence in personality interpretations and diagnoses, whether offered by lay people or mental health professionals.

Evil and illusion are not the *whole* story of our human condition. Although we may be but dust and ashes and tainted throughout by sin, we are also the image-bearers of God himself, the pinnacle of his creation. For our sake the world was created! Why, then, this dour preoccupation with human evil and illusory thinking? If we appreciated equally the grandeur and the depravity of human nature, there would be no need to concern ourselves with things so sinister. But, as we shall see, human selfishness and self-deceit produce a blindness to themselves. We tend to err on the side of optimism. People more readily perceive, remember, and speak pleasant rather than unpleasant information.[2] Since we tend naively to gloss over evil, especially in this age of humanism and material achievement, my emphasis on the pernicious side of human nature attempts only to help balance the picture.

There is benefit in bringing the suppressed truth to the surface. In the long run, truth usually provides a more durable foundation for comfort than does illusion. Seek truth first and you may eventually find comfort, advise the sages. Seek comfort first and, when the illusion crumbles, you will find despair. Since pride does generally go before a fall, we may avoid some catastrophes by keeping our self-appraisal in touch with reality. "Man will become better," noted Anton Chekhov, "only when you make him see what he is like." Those who fail to recognize that the proverbial glass is half-empty as well as half-full will be the last to take steps to keep the glass from going dry. As Reinhold Niebuhr concluded, "faith is always imperiled on the one side by despair and on the other side by optimism. Of these two enemies of faith, optimism is the more dangerous."[3]

Since evil and self-delusion are central to human existence, Part III asks, "Where Then Is Hope?" Unfortunately, our illusory thinking often makes us gullible to false hopes. In our age, false promises are offered most prominently by the multitude of manuals and programs which market self-redemption, by the advocates of mental health services, and by the glamorized exaggerations of popular religion. Christian faith, by contrast, proclaims something more significant than psychological adjustment. Its hope is not built on a make-believe image of human nature, nor does it promise relief from life's agonies. It incorporates the brute facts, yet responds to them with a good news message of hope and redemption. We need neither deny our propensity to selfishness, pride, and illusion, nor wallow in it. The good news of resurrection faith is that human evil will not have the last word; our valuing of ourselves can be anchored in something more substantial and lasting than the shaky ground of our own virtue and wisdom, and our vision of a new age to come gives hope and direction to our life here on earth.

PART ONE

THE DYNAMICS
OF EVIL

Human nature is bewildering. On the one hand we delight in the grandeur of the human mind and all its manifestations in science and the arts. It's easy to see that we do, indeed, reflect the very image of God. Yet as we scan our past and project our future we are dismayed. Our enormous capacity for compassion and reason seems equaled by our capacity for evil and illusion. Self-interest is the dominant motivation for most of us, although it is usually covered by a veneer of niceness. Occasionally the veneer wears thin and we glimpse what lies underneath. As Howard Jarvis, leader of the 1970s' tax rebellion succinctly put it, "It's them or us and we're for us."

The global implications of these human tendencies are alarming. Projecting the present rate of increase in nuclear weapons, energy consumption, and world population into the future suggests a dismal tomorrow for spaceship earth. And it is all the more frightening when we consider that on the time clock of human history this explosion in the human capacity for consumption and destruction has occurred in just the past few seconds. One is occasionally overwhelmed by a sense that things are out of control and careening toward disaster.

So it seems that while our species is favored with a unique potential for positive achievement, it is imperiled by its darker inclinations to a self-serving corruption of this potential. Perplexed by this mixed picture, we look to the new analyses of science and to the older traditions of religious wisdom for clearer insight into our human nature. How do science and religion understand our propensity to evil, and how well do their respective insights fit together?

In much the same way that the phenomena theologians call natural evil—earthquakes, tornadoes, and other natural disasters—can be understood and described by scientists, so too can the dynamics of human evil. The natural scientist offers explanations of natural evils that do not directly bear upon certain deeper theological questions about such phenomena, but the explanations do at least help us better understand the internal working of such evils. In a parallel manner, I shall draw from the human sciences a technical description of the workings of human evil. However, this will be more controversial than the natural scientist's description of natural evil. Claims made about human nature are claims made about your nature and mine, a subject about which you and I already have strong opinions.

I will use the term *human evil* in the everyday sense: actions done by men and women which harm people or which are self-serving at others' expense. After examining psychological theory and research concerning the roots of such actions, we will see how the psychological account squares with the biblical understanding of evil.

CHAPTER 1

A Psychology of Personal Evil

The psychological roots of human evil will be any inherent tendencies or external forces which are conducive to harming people, or to serving self at others' expense. Let's consider first some new scientific ideas concerning our personal selfishness and greed.

BASIC SELFISHNESS

A variety of psycholgical perspectives have long presumed that human beings are fundamentally selfish. Human behavior is typically explained in terms of reinforcement and punishment, pleasure and pain, benefits and costs, or the satisfaction and frustration of needs and drives. Economists and political scientists likewise assume that people act to maximize their own sense of well-being.

The controversial new science of sociobiology proposes a biological basis for these self-serving behavioral tendencies. For sociobiologists, selfishness is *genetic* selfishness—any act that contributes to the perpetuation of one's genes, be that action self-saving cowardice in battle or self-sacrifice on behalf of one's children. Throughout evolutionary history each new set of genes has competed with others for survival. Natural selection has presumably ensured that social behaviors that increase the chances of a gene's survival are most likely to be passed along to subsequent generations. An organism that indiscriminately sacrifices itself so that others may live is obviously less likely to have its genes perpetuated than an organism predisposed to self-saving selfishness. The brave young man who volunteers for the front line in battle and the hungry young woman who shares her meager food supply with strangers are less likely than those more selfish in their group to survive and pass on their genes. Thus if there is any genetic contribution toward selfish vs. altruistic modes of social behavior, we may presume that evolution would long ago have selected and perpetuated the self-saving tendencies. As La Rochefoucauld long ago surmised, virtues "lose themselves in selfish motives like rivers in the sea." Sociobiologist David Barash puts it more strongly: "Real, honest-to-God altruism simply doesn't occur in nature."

If human thought and action are biologically biased toward selfishness, then a corresponding social evolution may have balanced this tendency with concern for the group. Celibate love must be socially taught, because it's not hereditary. Donald Campbell has observed that many of the commandments such as "Love thy neighbor" and "Honor thy parents" command "tendencies that are in direct opposition to the 'temptations' which for the most part represent dispositional tendencies produced by biological evolution."[1] Since we are naturally disposed to "show independence from thy parents," there was little need to institute a rule for this.[2] This social counterforce to individual selfishness—which does occasionally produce real altruism in us humans—apparently developed because the ancients understood that individual well-being is undermined in the long run if the overall needs of the group are not served as well.

The sociobiological perspective on human nature is controversial, partly because it is conjecture, reasoned conjecture though it be. Those of us in social psychology prefer having conclusions also built upon actual behavior that we can observe. Can the supposed primacy of selfishness be demonstrated in laboratory experiments?

Social psychologists have examined self-interest vs. group-interest in laboratory games that pit the pursuit of immediate personal gain against the common good. The games are constructed in such a way that the pursuit of one's self-interest is detrimental to the group. To illustrate the logic of these games, imagine yourself in a group of six. I give you each a green chip, worth $15, and a white chip, worth $30, one of which you must choose to redeem for the cash. The catch is that I will fine everyone $5 for each white chip cashed in. What chip would you turn in? The rational strategy for maximizing your personal profit would be to turn in the white chip, which increases your profit by $15 minus the $5 fine. But if everyone does this, all end up making nothing, whereas everyone would have made $15 if all had turned in their green chips.

College students playing these games usually pursue their immediate self-interest. Cooperative behavior usually disappears because selfish behavior so easily takes advantage of it. The games parallel life. For example, pollution and depletion of natural resources are generally motivated by the lure of profit. A single industrial firm which encumbered itself with expensive pollution control procedures would not survive in the free market. In business, as in human evolution, competition for survival favors those who elevate their own interests above the community's interests. Hence in business, as in the evolution of societies, rules emerge which control the natural bias toward selfishness.

This idea of underlying selfishness registers a familiar ring from our daily experience. Who among us has not sensed it upon hearing of a competitor's misfortune? As La Rochefoucauld once observed, "In the misfortune of our dearest friends we always find something not entirely displeasing."

And have we not sensed the primacy of selfishness as people spend most of their energies on the personal concerns of themselves and their families, while world famine, tyranny, and nuclear weaponry proliferate and world resources are depleted?

GREED

This basic biological drive toward goals determined by self-interest is further complicated in human beings by psychological factors that make these drives fundamentally insatiable. Many Americans today think that their financial condition is far worse than it used to be. With rising inflation and taxes we complain that we no longer can afford what we used to buy routinely. When the bills come we bemoan that it's impossible to make ends meet.

Yet, despite all this "poortalk," the fact is that never have so many been so unthankful for so much.[3] The average American's buying power has actually seldom been higher. We know that consumer prices have more than doubled in the past 25 years, but we are less keenly conscious that our average income has more than tripled, enabling middle-class Americans to buy such wonderments as vehicles for "simple" recreation, facelifts to hide their aging, and hot tubs to soothe their anxious psyches. Even correcting for increased taxes as well as inflation, real disposable income has risen more than 50%.

Why, then, do we not *feel* 50% more affluent than we felt in the early 1950s? Why do yesterday's luxuries—color televisions, garage door openers, and stereo sound systems—become today's necessities, leading most people to feel that their needs are always slightly greater than their incomes? (This has been called Parkinson's Second Law: expenditures rise to meet income.) And what expressions of frustration and social conflict may we expect if, as many predict, the physical limits to economic growth usher in an era of no-growth economy, or even force us to simplify our lifestyles?

Psychological researchers have developed some principles

which help explain our insatiability. One principle, called the "adaptation-level" phenomenon, is well-grounded in recent research and dates back to the Epicurean and Stoic philosophers of ancient Greece. Its premise is that our feelings of success and failure, satisfaction and dissatisfaction, are relative to our prior achievements. If our current achievements are below the neutral point defined by prior experience, then we feel dissatisfied and frustrated; if they are above, then we feel successful and satisfied.

If the achievements continue, however, we soon adapt to the success. What was formerly positive is now only neutral, and what was formerly neutral becomes negative. This is why, despite the rapid increase in real income during the past several decades, the average American is not appreciably happier. The University of Michigan's Survey Research Center, for example, reports that in 1957 34% of Americans described themselves as "very happy." By 1978 our affluence had grown considerably, but, still, 34% said they were "very happy." Thus, concludes Donald Campbell, we humans could never create a social paradise on earth.[4] Once achieved, our utopia would soon be recalibrated, and we would again feel sometimes pleased, sometimes deprived, and sometimes neutral. Even Jacqueline Onassis can protest that "I'm not really that rich" (which reminds me of "Pardo's postulate": "Don't care if you're rich or not, as long as you can live comfortably and have everything you want").

Most of us have experienced the adaptation-level phenomenon. Increased material goods, meat, leisure time, or social prestige provides an initial surge of pleasure, but eventually that wanes and it takes an even higher level to give us another surge of pleasure. "Even as we contemplate our satisfaction with a given accomplishment, the satisfaction fades," note Campbell and colleague Philip Brickman, "to be replaced finally by a new indifference and a new level of striving."[5] As the drama of life unfolds, the one constant is that people, both young and old, sometimes feel up, sometimes down, and sometimes neutral.

A recent study of state lottery winners illustrates the adaptation-level principle.[6] Brickman and his colleagues found that people typically said that winning the lottery was one of the best things ever to have happened to them. Yet their self-reported overall happiness did not increase. In fact, ordinary activities, like reading or eating breakfast, became less pleasurable. Winning the lottery seemed to be such a high point that their ordinary pleasures paled by comparison.

Soon after his repatriation from the Shantung Compound, a World War II internment camp in China where 1500 foreigners had lived on a subsistence level diet, Langdon Gilkey accompanied his mother to the corner grocery. It was not a huge supermarket,

> And yet it completely overwhelmed me. I stood in the middle staring at those shelves piled high with food, cereals, breads, canned vegetables, fruit and meats, layer on layer of food, spilling over, piles of it in corners, and beyond the butcher's counter, there was more piled high in opened crates and boxes. I felt engulfed in food, drowned in immense and inexhaustible wealth, stuffed and bloated with so many fats, calories, and vitamins that I wanted to run outside. Meanwhile, people in the store were talking of their relief that the rigors of rationing were over. I understood then what real affluence meant. The break with our life in camp, which obviously still dominated my consciousness, seemed infinite.[7]

Our dissatisfactions bred by adapting to affluence are compounded when we compare ourselves with others. Ephraim Yuchtman (Yaar) has observed that feelings of well-being, especially among white-collar workers, are closely connected with the extent to which they feel compensated equitably with others in their line of work.[8] A salary raise for a city's police officers can temporarily lift their morale, yet may deflate that of the firefighters. Laboratory experiments indicate further that when people can compare themselves with others, they are more likely to compare themselves with those whose performance or rewards are ahead of theirs than with those beneath them.[9] Thus, feelings of "relative deprivation" frequently result from our comparisons with other people.

This phenomenon has a parallel in everyday life. As employees or families increase in affluence or social status, they raise the standards to which they compare and evaluate their own achievements. When climbing the ladder, people look up, not down. Their attention is on where they are going, not on where they have come from. This upward comparison further whets human appetites. But, unfortunately, the rungs go on forever. So unless we keep our feet on the ground, we will forever be climbing after and comparing ourselves with those above us. Better to choose the "former" and renounce the ladder.

The adaptation-level and relative deprivation principles have several thought-provoking implications. First, assuming that inequality of wealth persists, there is a real sense in which we shall "always have the poor."[10] The poor remain poor partly because the criteria for poverty are continually redefined.[11]

Second, seeking life satisfaction through material achievement requires a continually expanding level of affluence to maintain old levels of satisfaction. "Poverty," said Plato, "consists not in the decrease of one's possessions but in the increase of one's greed." In a report to his constituents, my congressman objected to a proposed tax on gas-guzzling cars because they are "driven by people who need large vehicles to pull boats or trailers." As a TV commercial declared, "When you want something bad enough it becomes a need."

Fortunately, the adaptation-level phenomenon should also enable us to adjust downward, should simplified lifestyles become a necessity. If our buying power shrinks, as it has at the end of the 1970s, we will feel some initial pain, but eventually we will adapt to that, too. In the aftermath of the 1970s gas price hikes, Americans have already managed to substantially reduce their appetite for big gas-slurping cars. Paraplegics, the blind, and other severely handicapped people generally adapt to their tragic situation and eventually recover a normal or near-normal level of life satisfaction. [12] Victims of traumatic accidents would surely exchange places with those who are not paralyzed, and most people would be delighted to win a state lottery. Yet, after a period of adjustment, none of these three groups differs appreciably from the other in moment-to-moment happiness. Human beings have an enormous adaptive capacity. As La Rochefoucauld recognized 300 years ago: "However great the discrepancies between men's lots, there is always a certain balance of joy and sorrow which equalizes all."

Finally, experiences that raise or lower our expectations may affect our level of satisfaction. Liberation movements, by raising their adherents' aspirations, can simultaneously stimulate increases in their achievements and decreases in their satisfaction. Becoming a feminist is probably *not* going to immediately alleviate a woman's frustration. In the short run, frustration is as likely to increase. On the other hand, situations which lower one's adaptation-level—through an experience of poverty or even, perhaps, of camping in the rough—can renew one's lost appreciation for former pleasures.

To sum up, when the continual recalibration induced by the adaptation-level phenomenon is joined by feelings of relative deprivation, greed results. Yesterday's wants become today's needs. And the result? "Poortalk" and insensitivity to the truly impoverished.

CHAPTER 2

A Psychology of Social Evil

We have so far considered the evil which arises from selfishness and from escalating aspirations. Some, locating human evil solely within the individual person, would have us stop here. If the defect is indeed personal, as American psychology and American religion have generally assumed, then the remedy is also personal: The way to alleviate unemployment is to put individuals through job training programs. The way to remedy emotional suffering is to put the individual in therapy. The way to deal with sin is to convert the individual.

But there is abundant evidence that the human problem is also corporate (and, as we shall later see, there is evidence that individualistic remedies usually deliver less than they promise). Evil emanates from the heart, the center, of the individual person, and yet it may also be seen as accumulating into a power which transcends and corrupts persons. Both history and science are replete with testimonies to the corrupting power of evil situations. We will pause to sample a vivid few.

EXTERNAL SOURCES OF EVIL

Evil situations can radically distort an entire culture. Dee Brown in his *Bury My Heart at Wounded Knee* describes how a changing situation provoked previously peaceful American Indian tribes into aggression and eventually into resignation. European traders offered the Iroquois tools, guns, and other goods for furs. As the forests shrank, the Iroquois' desire for these items brought them into competition with neighboring tribes, and their way of living changed from that of a hunting people with a subsistence economy to that of a warring nation.[1] Colin Turnbull's *The Mountain People* tells a similar story of how the peaceful, cooperative Ik people of northeastern Uganda, after being moved to a barren new region, were transformed into a "passionless, feelingless association of individuals."[2]

The miniature world of Langdon Gilkey's *Shantung Compound* provided a powerful portrayal of how evil can be unleashed by social circumstance. Although the prisoner-of-war camp housed many supposedly ethically sophisticated people—among them, missionaries, doctors, lawyers, and professors—living on bare essentials elicited a pervasive self-centeredness. The "fundamental bent of the total self in all of us was inward, toward our own welfare," observed Gilkey. "And so immersed were we in it that we hardly seemed able to see this in ourselves."[3] For example, when 1500 American Red Cross parcels were delivered to the camp without distribution instructions, the 200 Americans insisted that all the parcels should go to them; the 1250 hungry non-Americans argued just as vehemently that the new wealth should be distributed for the good of the whole community. As the conflict escalated, the parcels remained under guard while the community descended into bitter strife and resentment. The Americans, having numerous moral, legal, or religious justifications for their position, did not see this as an instance of their own selfishness. Some of the Americans argued that voluntarily donating a couple of the seven and one-half parcels each American was to receive would be more moral than would legislating sharing (translated: this way I can feel generous, yet still preserve most of my wealth; if the camp government distributes the wealth I feel neither righteous nor wealthy). Time and again during the

Shantung Compound experience, moral concern was but a veneer; whenever the security of the self was threatened, the veneer became transparent, exposing the underlying concern for self.

Laboratory experiments, though they usually lack the drama of daily life, enable us to isolate some of the important features of social situations and to examine their effects under controlled conditions. By compressing social forces into a brief time period, we can see how these forces affect people.

A number of experiments have put well-intentioned people in an evil situation to see whether good or evil prevails. The simplest experiments have exposed people to straightforward social pressure. To a dismaying extent, evil overwhelms good intentions, inducing people to conform to false standards or to capitulate to cruelty. Nice guys don't finish nice. Stanley Milgram's obedience experiments provide the best example.[4] Under optimum conditions—an imposing, close-at-hand commander and a remote victim—65% of his adult male subjects fully obeyed instructions to deliver what were supposedly traumatizing electric shocks to a screaming innocent victim in an adjacent room. These were regular people—a mix of blue collar, white collar, and professional men. They despised their task, yet most could not disengage themselves from it.

A significant feature of the obedience experiments was, I think, that the leader first asked the subjects to perform only a barely noticeable act of cruelty. The experimenter then began increasing his demands, each time eliciting a slightly greater cruelty. This subtle step-by-step entrapment is one of the most heinous dynamics of evil. The Nazis steadily escalated the cruelty their people inflicted on the Jews, and in similar fashion the Vietnam War was inexorably escalated. In everyday life as in the laboratory, obedience to authority often takes precedence over one's moral sense. The My Lai massacre demonstrated most tragically that evil deeds are sometimes not the product of unusually evil people acting from consciously malevolent motives, but of compliant people following orders.

The pathological potential of social situations is also evident in circumstances which do not coerce subjects with brute social pressure. Numerous studies indicate the powerful effects of occupying a social role, whether a temporary laboratory role or a long-term vocational or sex role. Although a new role may at first feel artificial—we can feel that we are "playing" it—the sense of phoniness soon begins to taper off as we absorb the role into our personalities and attitudes. Participating in destructive roles can therefore corrupt a person. Soldiers almost unavoidably develop positive images of themselves and degrading images of their enemy.

Philip Zimbardo's prison simulation illustrates this vicious process.[5] Among a volunteer group of decent young men, some were randomly designated guards; they were given uniforms, billy clubs and whistles, and were instructed to enforce certain rules. The remainder became prisoners, locked in barren cells and forced to wear a humiliating outfit. After a day or two of role "playing," the guards and prisoners, and even the experimenters, became caught up in the situation. The guards devised cruel and degrading routines, the prisoners either broke down, rebelled, or resigned, and the experimenters worked overtime to maintain prison security. This demonstration's prime lesson concerns not only the dehumanizing effects of guard-prisoner role relations. The steel bars symbolize how destructive role relations can affect rich and poor, white and black, husband and wife, employer and employee, teacher and student.

Competing for scarce goods—money, jobs, etc.—can also be destructive. It has long been recognized that prejudice is strongest when two groups conflict over mutually exclusive goals; an "us vs. them" mentality typically emerges. National surveys indicate that prejudice is strongest among groups that are close on the socioeconomic scale, apparently because they are in closest competition for jobs and housing. (This parallels the ecologists' principle that maximum competition occurs between species with identical needs.) Sophisticated white male collegians are not immune to the phenomenon when they believe that their admission to graduate or professional school is threatened by affirmative action programs for the recruitment of women and minorities.

In everyday situations many different factors are intertwined, so we cannot be sure that competition, in and of itself, is destructive. A number of creative experiments have therefore isolated the competition variable and tested its effects. In one of the most significant research programs ever undertaken in social psychology, Muzafer Sherif and his colleagues offered a summer camp experience to a large number of healthy, eleven- and twelve-year-old Midwestern American boys.[6] None of the boys knew each other. Sherif, after ascertaining what seemed to be the necessary conditions for hostility between groups, introduced these apparent essentials into this little world to see if the expected prejudice and violence would actually occur. First, he randomly separated the boys into two groups. For a time, they lived separately with their group and cooperated on various tasks, thus establishing their group identity. The groups were then brought together for a series of competitive activities. Since there were prizes to the winning team, one group could achieve its goal only by defeating the other group. Before long, the two groups were calling each other names, making derogatory posters, hurling food, and attacking each other with violence. It was warfare on a twelve-year-old scale, an experimental version of William Golding's *Lord of the Flies*. Recall the Americans and non-Americans contending for the Red Cross parcels. There too, competing for goals each party desired produced intense hostility. In Sherif's experiment, the conflict developed without any cultural, physical, or economic differences between the groups and with just ordinary boys taking part. The evil outcomes were a product of the transcendent power of an evil situation.

This experiment hints at the power of a group to intensify destructive tendencies, a power tragically evident in the murders and subsequent mass suicides by Jim Jones's People's Temple community in Guyana. Reinhold Niebuhr sensed this group power when he ascribed the "inferiority of the morality of groups" to "the revelation of a collective egoism, compounded of the egoistic impulses of individuals, which achieve a more vivid expression and a more cumulative effect when they are united in a common impulse than when they express themselves separately and discretely."[7] I, too, have noted this phenomenon. In my own study of "group polarization," I found that groups have a tendency to amplify the attitudes and behavior of the group's members.[8] When people talk over basically common views, their dominant feeling is likely to intensify. The group moves further in the direction of its members' dominant impulse. Several experimenters have found that when people are given a choice between behaving selfishly and altruistically (e.g., keeping some money for oneself or sharing it with others), group interaction generally amplifies selfishness, not only confirming Niebuhr's "collective egoism," but also indicating further the dominance of human selfishness.

This polarization effect contributes to conflict between groups. We have observed, for example, that when strongly prejudiced people discuss racial issues with other strongly prejudiced people, and when less prejudiced people do so with their own kind, they each reinforce their initial opinions. This further polarizes the two groups. Studies of campus unrest, gang delinquency, and community conflict provide real-life parallels to this. Group interaction may amplify conflict partly because, as we have observed in the laboratory, people when in groups are more inclined toward self-justification than when alone. Group pride is part of the "groupthink" process which Irving Janis proposed to help explain fiascoes in political decision, such as the escalation of the Vietnam War.[9]

When groups provide us with anonymity in a situation, they provoke the worst in us by enabling us to avoid accountability. Mobs can produce this result. So also can Halloween costumes, or even uniforms. In one experiment, young women were dressed in identical white coats and hoods, looking like members of the Ku Klux Klan. Asked to deliver electric shocks to a person, they did so with much more aggressiveness than did women who were not anonymous.[10]

Anonymity of a potential victim produces the same result, which is why slave owners and nations at war will dehumanize their victims. It is much easier to brutalize a nonperson than a person. Charles Manson and his family used the phrase "the Establishment" to depersonalize their victims. Likewise, when a victim of laboratory shocks or of a natural tragedy is distant, people act with much less compassion than when the victim is visibly close at hand. Alexander Solzhenitsyn, upon receipt of his Nobel Prize, lamented that when 200,000 people drowned in the Bangladesh tidal wave it gave most people less anguish than would a traffic injury to their neighbor. Those appealing on behalf of the unborn or of the hungry and impoverished in some distant land will therefore nearly always *personalize* the target groups with a compelling photograph of some individual.

This review only begins to identify the social sources of human evil. It leaves unmentioned factors involving the sociological situation or early childhood experiences and gives scant attention to the enormous research literature on the social and environmental determinants of human aggression.[11] I nevertheless trust that what is here is sufficient to remind us of the great corrupting power of evil situations. Like the seductive evil power of the ring, in Tolkien's *Lord of the Rings*, situational forces can override and even reshape one's basic values.

docum?

Every one of the social forces we have reviewed—malevolent authority, gradual escalation, conflicting roles, competition, group interaction, anonymity—can have significant destructive effects. Combining several of these ingredients will result in a social recipe for evil. Fortunately, reversing these conditions produces more admirable behavior. But that story is for a different book. *Yes, but doesn't the fact run against the thesis of this one.*

PRIDE

If, as I have argued, we are driven by an internal propensity toward selfishness and insatiable greed and are frequently corrupted by evil circumstance, then how do we live with ourselves? Many recent experiments consistently indicate that we tend to remember and analyze the events of our lives so as to take personal credit for desirable, positive happenings and to avoid blame for negative ones. Moreover, we generally come to morally justify acts we have committed. These self-serving and self-justifying tendencies manifest themselves both individually and collectively.

The Self-Serving Bias

During the 1970s, social psychology's most active research literature concerned "attribution"—how we explain our own and others' behavior. When do we attribute the cause of an action to the person—to the person's inner disposition, for example—and when do we attribute an action to external factors?

Time and again, experiments have revealed that people tend to attribute positive behaviors to themselves and negative behaviors to external factors, enabling them to take credit for their good acts and to deny responsibility for their bad acts.[12] The explanation for this phenomenon is being debated, but the reality and potency of the self-serving bias is not.[13] Although it is popularly believed that most people suffer from the "I'm not OK—you're OK" syndrome, research indicates that William Saroyan was much closer to the truth: "Every man is a good man in a bad world—as he himself knows."

A few sample experiments illustrate the phenomenon. A person trying to influence another (while playing the role of teacher or therapist) tends to take credit for a positive result, but to blame failure on the other.[14] Likewise, after working on a problem, people generally accept credit for their successes (attributing such to their ability and effort), yet attribute failures to external factors such as bad luck and the inherent difficulty of the task. Perhaps this is why games that combine skill and chance are popular. Winners can easily attribute their success to their skill while losers can just as easily attribute their loss to chance. When I win at Scrabble it's because of my verbal dexterity; when I lose it's because "who could get anywhere with a Q but no U?" My fourteen-year-old son recently won $25.00 by coming close to guessing the number of shoes stocked by a local shoe store. His guess was a wild stab in the dark. But upon hearing of his success, he immediately perceived himself a "skillful guesser," and announced that "From now on I'm going to enter all the guessing contests I can find."

In experiments that require two people to cooperate in order to make money, most individuals blame their partner when the couple fails to cooperate. This finding illustrates a tendency evident in that most ancient of attributions: Adam's excuse that "The woman you gave me . . ." Students exhibit this self-serving bias. Researchers have found that after receiving an examination grade, those who do well tend to accept personal credit by judging the exam as a valid measure of their competence. Those who do poorly are likely to criticize the exam as a poor indicator. [15]

When two people exhibit the self-serving bias—each blaming the other for bad deeds while excusing one's own—open hostility is not far away. It happens in marriage and in aggressive confrontations between police and citizens. Each party sees its own toughness as reasonable, but attributes the other's actions to an evil disposition. In marriage conflict, John attributes Mary's actions to her nastiness, but sees his own hostility as entirely justified. War crimes trials have thrown the principle of non-responsibility for evil into bold relief. One searches in vain for those who will step forward to accept accountability for the atrocities of Auschwitz or My Lai.

Michael Ross and Fiore Sicoly have observed the self-serving bias in several experiments. [16] In one, they interrupted couples talking in cafeterias and lounges and asked each person to estimate how much he or she had spoken during the conversation. On the average, each estimated having spoken 59% of the time. In other studies, the investigators found that married people usually felt they took more responsibility for such activities as cleaning the house and caring for the children than their spouses were willing to give them credit for. (My wife and I pitch our underclothes at our bedroom clothes hamper every night, and in the morning one of us puts them in. Recently she suggested that it would be nice if I took more responsibility for this. Thinking that I already did this 75% of the time, I asked her how often she thought she did it. "Oh," she replied, "about 75% of the time.") This bias needn't be consciously self-aggrandizing. Ross and Sicoly believe that the bias is due partly to the greater ease with which we recall things we have actively done, compared with the things we have not done.

These findings are complemented by research that consistently reveals that, on a variety of dimensions, most people see themselves as better than average. For example, most people see themselves as more ethical than their peers and as less prejudiced than most in their communities.[17] Los Angeles residents view themselves as healthier than most residents, and most college students believe they will outlive their actuarially predicted age of death by about ten years.[18] (It has been said that Freud's favorite joke was about the man who told his wife, "If one of us should die, I think I would go live in Paris.")

Jean-Paul Codol conducted twenty experiments with French people ranging from twelve-year-old schoolchildren to adult professionals.[19] Regardless of those involved and the experimental methods, the people's self-perceived superiority was present consistently. If given a teamwork task, people saw themselves as more cooperative than others; if given a competitive task, they perceived themselves as more competitive. Codol also found that the more people admired a particular trait, the more likely they were to see this trait as truer of themselves than of others.

You can demonstrate the self-serving bias by having a group of people anonymously indicate their standing on a variety of socially desirable traits. For example, ask those who drive whether they are better or worse than the average driver. Or have them compare themselves with others by filling in a blank: "My hunch is that about _____% of the others in this room are more *sympathetic* than I am." Bias seems to operate most freely when one is assessing subjective traits such as sympathy or morality on which objective comparison is difficult. On the fill-in-the-blank example, students typically rate themselves in the top of the class.

Each year the College Board invites the million high school seniors who take its aptitude test to indicate various things about themselves, including "how you feel you compare with other people your own age in certain areas of ability." Judging from their responses in the most recent year for which data are available, it appears that America's high school students are not racked with inferiority feelings. In "leadership ability," 70% rated themselves above average, two percent as below average. Sixty percent viewed themselves as better than average in "athletic ability," only 6% as below average. In "ability to get along with other," *zero* percent of the 829,000 students who responded rated themselves below average, 60% rated themselves in the top 10%, and 25% saw themselves among the top 1%! Consciously, at least, a "superiority complex" predominates over the inferiority complex.

Note how radically at odds this conclusion is with the popular wisdom that most of us suffer from low self-esteem and high self-disparagement. We are, to be sure, strongly motivated to maintain and enhance our self-esteem and we will welcome any message which helps us do that. But most of us are not groveling about with feelings that everyone else is better than we are. Preachers who deliver ego-boosting pep talks to audiences who are supposedly plagued with miserable self-images are preaching to a problem that seldom exists.

Oh, people do verbally disparage themselves, to be sure. Most of us have learned that putting ourselves down is a useful technique for eliciting "strokes" from others. We know that a remark like "Every time I see Carol in that beautiful dress, I wish I weren't so ordinary-looking" will elicit a comforting "Now Jane, don't say you're plain. You have gorgeous hair and your ponytail will soon be back in style."

Of course, not everyone suffers equally from the self-serving bias. Some people *do* suffer from unreasonably low self-esteem. (Such people are somewhat more likely to seek out the very psychologists who, based on their impression of their clients, tell us that the basic human problem is low self-esteem.) And even the many more people who exhibit the self-serving bias may still feel inferior to certain specific individuals, especially when they compare themselves with individuals who are a step or two higher on the ladder of success.

Self-serving perceptions are not conscious lies; they are self-deceptions. In fact, there may be functional wisdom in this pride. Constant striving to prove our superiority can drive us to achieve. The self-serving bias may also sustain our sense of hope and purpose. One recent study found that while most people see themselves more favorably than other people see them (thus exhibiting the "normal" self-serving bias), depressed people see themselves *as* others see them.[20] So we had best not take an ax to people's illusions unless we have a more solid hope to offer in exchange.

Some sociobiologists have even suggested that self-deception has been selected by natural evolution; cheaters, for example, may give a more convincing display of honesty if they believe in their honesty. Being ignorant of one's selfishness and pride may have had survival value. For this reason, concludes Donald Campbell, "moral intuitions are to be distrusted when applied to one's own behavior."[21] La Rochefoucauld, whose witty and perceptive *Maxims* (1665) expose the manifestations of self-interest and pride, also believed pride serves a function: "It seems that Nature, which has so wisely constructed our bodies for our welfare gave us pride to spare us the painful knowledge of our shortcomings."

However, the self-serving bias is not always adaptive. An impressive series of experiments by Barry Schlenker shows how self-serving perceptions can poison a group.[22] In nine different experiments Schlenker had people work together on some task, and then receive false information suggesting their group had done either well or poorly. In every one of these studies the members of successful groups claimed more responsibility for their group's performance than did members of groups who supposedly failed at the task. The same self-congratulatory tendency surfaced, although not quite as strongly, when people compared themselves with others in their own groups. Unless their conceit could be publicly debunked, most presented themselves as contributing more than the others when the group did well; few said they contributed less.

Such self-deception can be detrimental in a group by leading its members to expect greater-than-average rewards (pay or otherwise) when their organization does well, and less-than-average blame when it doesn't. If most individuals in a group believe they are underpaid and underappreciated, relative to their better-than-average contributions, disharmony and envy are likely. College presidents will readily recognize the phenomenon. If, as one survey revealed, 94% of college faculty think themselves better than their average colleague, then when merit salary raises are announced and half receive an average raise or less, many will feel an injustice has been done them. Note that the complaints do not necessarily signify that any actual injustice has been done. Even if, unknown to the employees, God himself had determined the raises according to his most perfect justice, discontent would likely still exist.

The resentment that accompanies high inflation—even in a time when wage increases keep pace with prices—partly reflects this self-serving bias. Economist George Katona has observed that people tend to perceive their wage increases as the return for their talent and effort, and hence see price increases as cheating them of gains which are rightfully theirs.[23]

Biased self-assessments can also distort managerial judgment. Corporation presidents widely predict more growth for their own than for competing firms and production managers similarly overpredict their performance.[24] As investigator Laurie Larwood has observed, such overoptimism can produce disastrous consequences. If those who deal in the stock market or in real estate perceive their business intuition to be superior to their competitors', they may be in for some severe disappointments.

We educators are prone to the same bias. The number of college-age young Americans will shrink nearly 25% between 1980 and the early 1990s. College officials realize that college enrollments nationwide are therefore to decline. Few, however, are planning how to cope with this on their own campuses. They figure rightly that even in a time of decline not all colleges will shrink. And since their schools are better than average they expect their own institutions to be among the fortunate few. This positive thinking undoubtedly will characterize administrators of colleges that *do* continue to thrive. Let's not underestimate the power of positive thinking. However, college officials who gaze at the future of their institutions through better-than-average rose-colored glasses may pay a price for their lack of better-than-average contingency planning.

When Larwood also surveyed people in a Northeastern city, she found that most thought they were more concerned than their fellow citizens about ensuring clean air and water and believed they used less electricity than the other residents. These average citizens were self-proclaimed better-than-average citizens. As Larwood notes, if most people "are merely the average persons that they must be statistically, but behave as though they are superior, their goals and expectations must inevitably conflict." For example, each will continue to use more than his or her fair share of resources.

See note on 37

Self-Justification

Many laboratory experiments have also explored the *consequences* of immoral action. Lying, cheating, or inflicting pain in laboratory experiments yields temporary discomfort, but self-esteem remains resilient. People will relieve the discomfort either by, if convenient, doing something to redeem themselves, or by rationalizing their action.[27] Not only do people tend to take credit for success and deny blame for failure, they also often come to deny the evil of acts they cannot disown.

Self-justification occurs because our attitudes and beliefs often *follow* our behavior. No generalization has been more firmly established during the last two decades of social psychological research.[28] For example, people who during an experiment are induced to give witness to something about which they have doubts will generally begin to believe their little lies, assuming they felt some sense of choice in the matter. Likewise, harming someone—by saying something hurtful or delivering electric shocks—usually leads aggressors to derogate their victim, especially if the harm-doing was coaxed rather than coerced. Evil acts shape the self. When an evil action is induced by subtle social forces this action begins to corrode the moral sensitivity of the actor. Thus the *external* sources of evil seductively feed the *internal* moral numbness that helps make the next evil act possible. This process seemed to be at work in Stanley Milgram's obedience experiments, described earlier, and it most certainly contributed to the moral justifications that perpetuated the Vietnam War.

The best-known explanation for this tendency to believe in what we have done is "cognitive dissonance theory." In recent years the theory has evolved into a theory of self-justification, explaining how beliefs get modified so as to maintain one's self-image.[29] People will go to great lengths to justify their action, be it the Khmer Rouge depopulating Cambodia, profit-lusting corporations convincing Third World mothers to abandon breast feeding for infant formula, or any one of us committing some lesser evil of everyday life. President Nixon's lies and deceit thus became mere "mistakes" and "misjudgments."

The most powerful justifications are moral and religious.

Freud, in *Civilization and Its Discontents*, argued that human destructiveness reaches its highest levels when the superego is enlisted in its service. Indeed, most evil is done by people who feel they have some permission or approval for what they do. Prayer services in support of the Hiroshima bombing crew, the Vietnam War, and the white-ruled governments of South Africa provide vivid examples. In seventeenth-century America the commonest way to indicate the distinction between black and white was to speak of Negroes and Christians.[30] If God himself sanctifies an event or an institution, then who would dare oppose it?

In the Shantung Compound, people constantly hid self-interest behind "moral principle" and religion. Although stealing from the camp's meager meat supply deprived one's already impoverished comrades, it became "patriotic" to do so since this was also stealing from the Japanese captors. Perhaps Rousseau was right in suggesting that pride is the spiritual corruption of the animal survival impulse "which leads every animal to look to its own preservation."[31] "The experiences of camp life, and the lessons of history generally," concluded Gilkey,

> established to my satisfaction that men act generally in an "immoral" way when their interests are at stake. With equal force, however, they showed me that men remain at least moral enough to be hypocritical, to wish to *seem* good—even if it is beyond their capacities to attain it.[32]

As Karl Menninger has noted, all slayers find justification for their act. "Hitler had his reasons for killing the Jews. Custer had his reasons for killing the Sioux. Our military men had reasons for killing Viet Cong soldiers, and the Viet Cong had their reasons for killing ours."[33]

Education and culture do not exempt one from the phenomenon. Within the memory of many still living today, 10 million innocent people, mostly Jews and Russians, were herded into boxcars and shipped off to be gassed to death or to be worked, starved, and tortured—in one of the most educated and supposedly civilized nations on earth. After a hard day's work, the camp commanders at Auschwitz would relax to the music of Beethoven and Schubert. The demonic and the angelic are intermixed deep in the lives of us all, whether European, Asian, African, or American, whether educated and "cultured" or not.

Collective Pride

As noted previously, group interaction often accentuates the tendencies of individual group members. If pride is as fundamental to human existence as research on the self-serving bias and self-justification suggests, then its manifestation in corporate settings is all the more fraught with diabolical potential. Irving Janis has noted that one source of destructive international conflict is the tendency of both sides to believe in the inherent morality of their acts.[34] Americans say that the United States builds missile bases near the Russian border in Turkey to protect the free world from Communism, and insist that the Soviet Union puts missiles in Cuba to threaten our security. And how do the Soviets view such events? They, of course, believe the motivation behind the building of their bases is self-protective while the United States' motivation is aggressive.

Janis documents from several historical fiascoes, such as the U.S. involvement in the Vietnam War, the ways in which group discussion can magnify self-righteousness. Group pressure in cohesive decision-making groups will often domesticate the dissenters. This gives an illusion of unanimity, inflating the group's confidence in the morality and effectiveness of its plans. Group members reinforce one another's shared stereotypes of the enemy, often leading themselves to view the enemy in such dehumanized terms that atrocity becomes sanctioned. For these reasons, self-justification associated with group harm-doing seems even stronger than when an individual acts alone. As the Nazis demonstrated, group pride has been a source of history's worst evils.

Americans have likewise been prone to see themselves as good and to locate evil elsewhere. Politicians cater to this group pride. Richard Nixon declared in his first inaugural address that "I know the heart of America is good," and Jimmy Carter based much of his 1976 campaign on the supposed goodness of the American people. This national pride has its darker side. As Freud recognized long ago, the denial of evil in oneself and one's group leads one to see evil in others and to justify their oppression. Black Americans have historically been stereotyped with those tendencies least fitting the Protestant ideal. Self-righteous feelings have therefore rationalized many a violent act against them. Likewise when the Marxist locates evil in the "enemies of the people," almost any aggression against them becomes justified.

Group pride is conducive to evil for yet another reason. Groups that manifest a proud "we feeling" will almost inevitably manifest a corresponding "they feeling." The social definition of who we are implies a definition of who we aren't. The ardent conviction that black or white—or American or Chinese, or male or female, or evangelical or liberal—is beautiful implies that its opposite is not. The nearly inevitable cost of a strong social identity is an increased gulf separating oneself from the out-group.

One of the clearest symptoms of collective pride is therefore prejudice, which is largely a group phenomenon. Since status is relative, a group needs someone below it in order to perceive itself as worthy. One psychological benefit of racism, or any social caste system, is the feeling of superiority which it offers. When a group agrees on the undesirability of some other group, the comparison boosts its self-esteem. If that other race or sex or nationality is inferior, then one's own is superior. Since proud people are always looking down on things and people, their pride, as C. S. Lewis recognized, is

> spiritual cancer: it eats up the very possibility of love. . . . Pride is *essentially* competitive—is competitive by its very nature—while the other vices are competitive only, so to speak, by accident. Pride gets no pleasure out of having something, only out of having more of it than the next man. We say that people are proud of being rich, or clever, or good-looking, but they are not. They are proud of being richer, or cleverer, or better-looking than others. If everyone else became equally rich, or clever, or good-looking there would be nothing to be proud about.[34]

Proper pride? (μεγαλοψυχία)

CHAPTER 3

A Theology of Evil

The dynamics of evil observed by research psychologists will come as no surprise to those familiar with the biblical story of our human condition, for the unfolding scientific picture of human nature reaches back in time to connect with this ancient view. Seeing the parellels between the scientific and biblical ideas may therefore renew our appreciation for the significance of the biblical idea, prompt us to sharpen and clarify its meaning, and open us to a deeper grasp of the biblical message of hope. Increasingly, the biblical image of sin and evil seems not to be archaic nonsense, as modern minds have so often supposed.

Our theological terminology may be archaic, but what matters is not so much the words as the reality to which they point. In dispensing with words like sin we have, however, thrown the baby out with the bathwater. Our sinful predicament is no longer preached from the major pulpits of the lands, and the old idea of sin has been converted into the modern idiom of symptom. A presidential candidate shocks the land by confessing sinful lust in his heart, and our Presidential Prayer Breakfasts are usually kept innocent of any mention of our collective sin.

Although our toes may curl at the mention of human sinfulness, it is increasingly evident that this biblical idea has a profound empirical reality. Although the psychological account of evil overlaps with the theological account, and helps substantiate the credibility of it, it does not duplicate or displace the theological account. Psychological researchers explore how evil operates in daily life. The biblical story of human evil moves to a deeper level in portraying evil as a spiritual problem. Theology is free to draw upon both the scientific and biblical revelations. Therefore, let us briefly look at how Christian theologians have understood the spiritual *root* of the problem. Doing so will prepare us to see if the expected *manifestations* of the problem fit with the scientific observations noted earlier.

THE ROOT OF THE PROBLEM

The Bible portrays us as creatures of ultimate value who are blessed with a great potential for love and wisdom. Yet, it also portrays us as created, dependent creatures. Our earthly existence is temporary, our wisdom is finite, our life is precarious. We are helpless infants, brief blips in the vast, timeless universe. In the face of this, where shall we find meaning and significance? Where lies our security? Christians believe that meaning and security are to be found by centering our lives on God, the source of our being.

Our inevitable response, however, is to declare our independence from God. Our need for meaning and security thus compels us to clutch at false, finite securities. Doing so is said to be the root of sin. "Sin," Reinhold Niebuhr wrote, "is occasioned precisely by the fact that man refuses to admit his 'creatureliness' and to acknowledge himself as merely a member of a total unity of life."[1] Its result is that we are all susceptible to the words of the Serpent: "You will be like God."[2] Sin is thus estrangement from God and devotion to finite realities—our career, our groups, our children, or any of many other such idols.

If this is indeed the root of the spiritual problem, its implications are profound. First, sin is not peripheral to our existence: the corruption emanates from the very core of our being as we center our existence on false securities. In

Scripture this implication appears in Jesus' teaching that evil comes from the heart, the center of our being.[3] Theologically, this appears in the doctrine of original sin, the idea that all of our existence is touched by our worshiping false idols. This religious understanding that evil is inherent in us—an inevitable corruption of our nature—is now paralleled by the scientific idea that selfishness, escalating greed, and the other social and cognitive sources of evil are intrinsic to our biological and social existence.

THE MANIFESTATIONS OF THE PROBLEM

Although, theologically, sin is our idolatrous attachment to false securities, its psychological manifestation is self-centeredness and pride. Langdon Gilkey put it this way:

> Injustice to other men, as Reinhold Niebuhr has said, is the social consequence of an inward idolatry, the worship of one's own self or group. The moral problems of selfishness, the intellectual problems of prejudice, and the social problems of dishonesty, inordinate privilege, and aggression are all together the result of the deeper religious problem of finding in some partial creature the ultimate security and meaning which only the Creator can give.
>
> This then is the religious meaning of sin, far different from the usual meaning given it by the legalist mentality. Sin may be defined as an ultimate religious devotion to a finite interest; it is an overriding loyalty or concern for the self, its existence and its prestige, or for the existence and prestige of a group. From this deeper sin, that is, from this inordinate love of the self and its own, stem the moral evils of indifference, injustice, prejudice, and cruelty to one's neighbor, and the other destructive patterns of actions that we call "sins."[4]

The spiritual center of our life, the object of our ultimate concern, is ourselves. Our moral concern for the well-being of others therefore recedes when this central concern is threatened, and we adjust our sense of what is rational and fair accordingly. The opposite of this self-serving and self-justifying tendency is the biblical ethic of self-giving love, exhibited in God's acts toward the Israelites and incarnated in Jesus' concern for others.

Pride follows on the Achilles' heel of self-centeredness. The tragic flaw portrayed in Greek drama was pride, "hubris." Like the subjects of our historical and laboratory experiments, the Greek tragic figures do not self-consciously choose evil, but rather think too highly of their own wisdom, thus producing disaster for themselves and others. They fail to recognize their limitations. In the biblical account, pride is self-deceit, ignorance of the truth about ourselves. In John's Gospel, the religious leaders are portrayed as blind, self-righteous teachers who typify our unwillingness to come to the light, lest our hypocrisy be seen. The experimental evidence that human reason is adaptable to self-interest is thus entirely congenial to the Christian contention that becoming aware of our own sin is like trying to see our own eyeballs: There are self-serving and self-justifying biases in the way we perceive our actions, observes the social psychologist; "No one can see his own errors," notes the Psalmist.[5] We cannot see our pride, because our pride prevents our seeing it. Thus the Pharisee could thank God "that I am not like other men" (or at least a better than average sinner).

The social psychological conclusion that pride has social consequences, such as prejudice, also echoes a biblical theme. Reinhold Niebuhr has noted that the prophets unfailingly "combined their strictures against the religious sin of pride and the social sin of injustice."[6] The social effects of pride make it basic among the "seven deadly sins." One modern prophetic voice who understands the social consequences of pride is Henry Fairlie:

Pride may excite us to take too much pleasure in ourselves, but it does not encourage us to take pleasure in our humanity, in what is commonly shared by all of us as social beings. The turning in to ourselves has turned us away from our societies. It is a sin of neglect: It causes us to ignore others. It is a sin of aggression: It provokes us to hurt others. It is a sin of condescension: It makes us patronize others. All of these are turned against our neighbors, and often in our Pride we do not realize how aloof we have become, and how cut off even from what in our own nature we should most deeply know and enjoy.[7]

Collective pride, as Niebuhr went on to observe, is probably the worst manifestation of sin, since through it whole peoples succumb to racism, sexism, nationalism, and other forms of idolatrous pretension. The Old Testament prophets continually had to challenge Israel's national pride, including her identification of God with country.

The social psychological insight regarding collective evil is paralleled by this biblical insight regarding collective evil. The external sources of evil noted earlier are represented in the story of the fall as Eve is seduced by an external demonic force. The social character of sin is also evident in Cain's murder of Abel, in Noah's drunkenness, in the foolishness of Babel, and in the Old Testament concept of the corporate personality—whole families and whole cities are sometimes condemned for their wickedness. New Testament images of "principalities and powers" reinforce the notion that evil transcends individuals, the book of Revelation offering perplexing images of bestial political powers.[8]

If there is a corporate aspect to sin, then there must be also a corporate response to it. Judaism and Christianity are distinguished, not by the mystical visions of spiritual isolates, but by a community life. Since we are not self-sufficient individual agents, we stand in need of the church's corporate fellowship as we struggle with the evil within and about us. It is the whole believing people that is the "Body of Christ," not isolated believers. To say the church is Christ's body reminds us that together we can admonish one another, we can enable each other to minister, and we can accomplish what we as individuals never could.

Social psychology seems to have dusted off some ancient

originally the 1/2 pgs fll. must have come in on 27. The fn. numbering is still 50.

wisdom about our human condition. The self-serving bias is the social psycholgist's new rendition of the forever underappreciated truth about human pride. St. Paul must have had this natural tendency in mind when he admonished the Philippians to "in humility count others better than yourselves."[25]

Yet, the true end of humility is not self-contempt (which still leaves people concerned with themselves). To paraphrase C. S. Lewis, humility does not consist in handsome people trying to believe they are ugly, and clever people trying to believe they are fools. When we hear a Nobel laureate respond to an interviewer with, "Well, Ted, yes, I was surprised, pleased even, when I heard the news. Actually, I'd have to consider myself no more than a better-than-average nuclear bioorganic microecological physical chemist," we may wonder where that leaves those of us who have a hard time following a recipe for pound cake.

When Muhammad Ali announced that he was the greatest, there was a sense in which his pronouncement did not violate the spirit of humility. False modesty can actually lead to an ironic pride in one's better-than-average humility. (Perhaps some readers have by now congratulated themselves on being unusually free of the inflated self-perception this book is describing.)

True humility is more like self-forgetfulness than false modesty. It leaves people free to rejoice in their special talents and, with the same honesty, to recognize their neighbor's. Both the neighbor's talents and one's own are recognized as gifts and, like one's height, are not fit subjects for either inordinate pride or self-deprecation. Ali's self-preoccupation did violate this aspect of humility, for in that ideal state there is neither vainglory nor false modesty, only honest self-acceptance.

As we have seen, true humility is a state not easily attained. "There is," said C. S. Lewis, "no fault which we are more unconscious of in ourselves. . . . If anyone would like to acquire humility, I can, I think, tell them the first step. The first step is to realize that one is proud. And a biggish step, too." The way to take this first step is to glimpse the greatness of God and see oneself in light of this, continued Lewis. "He and you are two things of such a kind that if you really get into any kind of touch with Him you will, in fact, be humble, feeling the infinite relief of having for once got rid of [the pretensions which have] made you restless and unhappy all your life."[26]

IS SIN A NECESSITY OF NATURE?

Our inquiry into the coherence of the psychological and theological accounts of evil has left us with one point at which these two perspectives on the human puzzle seem not to fit together. The scientific perspective sees evil as a by-product of our biological and social nature. But in the biblical account, sin is a deviation from an originally good human nature, a defacement of the image of God. The fall comes after the creation, making *us* responsible, not God. Although the sociobiological notion of genetically disposed selfishness may in some sense parallel Augustine's notion of inherited corruption, most theologians squirm at the suggestion that sin is a natural product of our biological and social evolution.

But one has an equally hard time making any *scientific* sense out of the theological idea that sin is a perversion of our created nature, not an essential characteristic of it. One way out of the dilemma is to presume that the myth of original goodness is without historical reality, being simply an abstract ideal of what humanity should strive to become or a concept of what it might be were it not for its corruption. But if selfishness and pride are intrinsic to creation, as the scientific account suggests, then, as Alvin Plantinga has wryly observed,

> Original sin must be laid to God's door. God is responsible. . . . Part of the ground rules of such a discussion is that one doesn't say that God thought it would be nice to have some sin. Or that just as God brought about natural laws, He brought about man's sin. The task is to find an expression for the origin of sin that is consistent with the holy character of God. [9]

(The same problem exists with explaining death, which in the Christian view is God's enemy, but in the natural scheme is essential for the elaboration of life.)

Resolutions of the problem have been attempted, but none are completely satisfying. For example, it has been suggested that the fall became possible in history when humanity evolved into self-consciousness and attempted to establish its own significance apart from God. Thus, perhaps we moved from innocence to responsibility and to the potential for separation from God when we became capable of reflecting on our actions and therefore of knowing good from evil.

It might also be observed that the dynamics of evil discussed here are by-products of a healthy, beautiful creation. The evolutionary perspective prompts the thought that just as death, our great enemy, made possible the elaboration of life, so also selfishness is a consequence of a fitness-producing natural system. The constant striving induced by the adaptation-level phenomenon gives human life its vitality; thus while our insatiability imprisons our hearts, leads us to injustice, and separates us from God, it also helps motivate human achievement. Although collective pride may be the root of much evil it has another side—an admirable loyalty to one's family, group, or nation. One of the great ironies of existence is that the conditions that make evil possible are sometimes the very conditions which made the good in creaturely life as we know it. Thus there is a real sense in which human evil may be seen as the flip side of a very good created order; without the "evil" we would not have the good. Wilhelm Leibnitz even carried this so far as to suggest that a world without evil would not have been as good as one with some evil, since so many "goods" are related to certain evils. Among some Christians this view surfaces in the claim that whatever happens—the death of a child, the loss of one's job, the breakup of a relationship—it is God's will and hence a net good, even if at the moment we can't always see the good. But surely, although some good can indeed be salvaged from the most evil happenings, this world is *not* the best of all possible worlds.

Perhaps we should not expect the biblical and scientific accounts of sin's origins to completely coincide, for these are different perspectives with utterly different purposes. The biblical account of the fall was not intended as literal history but as a supra-scientific truth. The first eleven chapters of Genesis affirm—in the Garden of Eden story, in Cain's murder of Abel, in the story of Noah, in the Tower of Babel—that sin is pervasive, hence the need for divine initiative in redemption. S. J. De Vries observes in the *Interpreter's Dictionary of the Bible* that the Old Testament

> writers were more concerned to trace the source of sin "existentially" in human life than to indulge in historical and cosmological speculations. The notion that it arises either from creatureliness as such or from sexual generation does not appear in the OT. Such passages as Job 14:1; 15:14; Ps. 51:5 . . . speak only of the fact that man is sinful from the time of conception and that frail "flesh" is prone to all the evils of life.[10]

Although psychological research cannot speak to the religious origins of human sin, descriptions of the present dynamics of evil *do* connect with biblical claims about our present state. The Genesis story, for whatever else it may be—be it literal truth, be it a nonliteral account of actual history, or be it mythical truth—is first of all the Bible's depiction of our human condition. It captures the saga of prideful self-assertion and its alienating effect upon our relationship with one another and with God. Regardless of whether the Genesis story also portrays an actual historical sequence, it at least suggests a universal history. Adam is the prototypical human, Everyman, the archetype of human experience. His underlying self-concern is ours; it "lies below our particular thoughts and acts, molds them, directs them, and then betrays us into the actual misdeeds we all witness in our common life."[11]

 Jesus, the prophets, and the whole biblical witness, therefore, challenge us to a higher honesty. Although recognizing our condition does not eliminate it, an honest glimpse at our selfishness and pride may at least put some brakes on rampant egocentricism and hypocrisy. And more than this, since the gospel takes up where the story of human evil leaves off, it may also lead us to believe, to enjoy, and to celebrate the liberating good news of our true hope and security.

PART TWO

ILLUSIONS OF HUMAN THOUGHT

What a piece of work is man! how
noble in reason! how infinite
in faculty! . . . in apprehension
how like a god.

WILLIAM SHAKESPEARE

We are the hollow men
We are the stuffed men
Leaning together
Headpiece filled with straw

T. S. ELIOT

Our human predicament stems not only from our vulnerability to external and internal pressures toward evil, but also from the foibles and fallacies of our thinking. New research in cognitive and social psychology is reminding us that human wisdom is, as St. Paul indicated, not nearly so wise as God's foolishness. Our limited reason is not inclined to understand its own limits, and this renders us susceptible to all sorts of sincere but erroneous beliefs.

Becoming aware of our gullibility and self-deception can be disillusioning. Nevertheless, my conviction is that a world view built on a make-believe image of human nature will ultimately lead to greater disillusionment than will a view that recognizes the hard truth and responds to it with a word of hope. Not only can the biblical understanding of human nature accommodate the experimental testimonies to the finiteness of the human mind, it expects them. In the biblical view, there is a vast gulf between the mind of God and that of us. There is nothing wrong with our being finite; the problem comes in the denial of our limits. Part of human evil, Reinhold Niebuhr once wrote, lies in the "effort to pretend a virtue and knowledge which are beyond the limits of mere creatures."

An explanation of how people arrive at unfounded convictions no more means that all convictions are unfounded than does explaining how people make counterfeit money mean that all money is counterfeit. But if one were to claim that counterfeit money abounds (as I shall claim that counterfeit beliefs abound) one would seek to explain how this happens. Knowing how illusory beliefs happen does not eliminate them

45

much more than does knowing about visual illusions liberate us from erroneous perceptions. However, understanding the frailty of our wisdom may at least move us to a clearer way of thinking about our thinking. It may, for example, help mute our arrogance and amplify our humility. Moreover, understanding common illusory thought processes can enhance our ability to scrutinize critically the whirlpool of conflicting ideas swirling constantly about us.

CHAPTER 4

How We Form and Sustain False Beliefs: I

The grandeur of the human intellect and its capacity for abstract reasoning is evident as we enjoy the achievements of modern technology and as we observe our own thinking. The limits to our thinking are less obvious. Thus we need to be reminded that, contrary to Hamlet's paean of praise, we are not always "noble in reason" and certainly not "infinite in faculty." Although the new experiments on illusory thinking are unprecedented, their conclusions are not entirely novel. More than 350 years ago, the English philosopher Francis Bacon described the deep fallacies of the mind as "idols of the tribe." We shall stand before a sampling of these idols in the following pages.

From its beginnings, psychology has explored the mind's amazing ability to fabricate experiences—dreams, hallucinations, perceptual illusions, and hypnotically induced delusions. For example, Sigmund Freud proposed that the "pleasure principle" is satisfied through our illusions, with the result that we often invent false arguments to support our illusions. As Calvin Hall has written, "Freud unmasked our hypocrisies, our phony ideals, our rationalizations, our vanities, and our chicaneries, and not all the efforts of humanists and rationalists will restore the mask."[1]

An artificially constructed belief about reality feels much like an objectively correct belief. Biopsychologist Jerre Levy recounts an experiment with patients whose two brain hemispheres had been surgically separated. When the right

47

how?

half of a girl's face was projected to the patients' nonverbal right hemispheres and the left half of a *woman's* face was projected to their verbal left hemispheres, they confidently *pointed* to a completed picture of the girl to identify the picture seen, but *said* they saw a woman. Each hemisphere invented the missing half face. Apparently the invented image was experienced the same as an objectively correct belief.

Past studies of human problem solving provide further evidence concerning the bounds of our ability to reason clearly. Consider the classic "horse-trading" problem:

> A man bought a horse for $60 and sold it for $70. Then he bought the same horse back for $80 and again sold it, for $90. How much money did he make in the horse business?

The answer (see footnote 2) may be obvious to you, but most American college students incorrectly answer even so simple a question as this. (A German university colleague informs me that most German banking executives also miss this one.)

The most unambiguous evidence concerning the formation of false beliefs comes, however, not from the speculations of Freud or the classic experiments of early American psychology, but from the vast new research literature on how our minds process information. I would predict that history will judge these new revelations as among psychology's most important contributions to human self-understanding— except that the very results which prompt me to suggest that also compel me to be cautious about making such bold judgments. Herbert Simon (who in 1978 became the first psychologist to win a Nobel Prize) was among the modern researchers who first described the bounds of human reason:

> The first consequence of the principle of bounded rationality is that [a person] construct[s] a simplified model of the real situation in order to deal with it. He behaves rationally with respect to this model, [but] such behavior is not even approximately optimal with respect to the real world. [3]

In Part I, I noted one example of bounded rationality: a self-serving bias in the way we perceive ourselves and others. Far from being impartial spectators, we explain and interpret events in self-serving ways. Reason easily becomes rationalization. This egocentric bias is but one of the many biases and imperfections in human thinking. Let us consider more.

WE OFTEN DO NOT KNOW WHY
WE DO WHAT WE DO

There is one thing, and only one in the whole universe which we know more about than we could learn from external observation. That one thing is Man. We do not merely observe men, we *are* men. In this case we have, so to speak, inside information; we are in the know.[4]

The truth of this observation by C. S. Lewis is self-evident; some things we know best by intuition and personal experience. The *fallibility* of our self-knowledge is, however, considerably less self-evident; sometimes we *think* we are "in the know," but our inside information is demonstrably erroneous. This is the unavoidable conclusion of some fascinating recent research.

A number of experiments have asked people why they did what they did and then compared their introspections with objective evidence indicating what *really* influenced them. People readily proclaim why in a particular situation they have felt or acted as they have. Yet, when the influences are not obvious, people are poor judges of their own behavior and its sources. In many different kinds of experiments, people whose actions were significantly altered by an experimental manipulation have denied that they have been influenced.[5] For example, if people's attitudes change during an experiment they often are unaware of it. Thus, when asked to recall their pre-experiment attitude, they believe that how they now feel is how they have always felt. Reports from Israel during the euphoric aftermath of the 1977 Begin-Sadat summit meeting indicated that many Israelis were claiming they had long felt affinity with the Egyptians, who had always been "different" from the other Arab countries. Observers of Israel say this self-perception is false—previously, Jordan and Lebanon were regarded most favorably. [6]

When confronted with the fact of their changed behavior, people often still cannot recognize what has influenced them. Richard Nisbett and Stanley Schachter demonstrated this by asking people to take a series of electric shocks of steadily increasing intensity. [7] Beforehand, some of the people were given a false pill which, they were told, would produce feelings of heart palpitations, breathing irregularities, and butterflies in the stomach—the very symptoms that usually accompany being shocked. Nisbett and Schachter anticipated that the people would therefore attribute these symptoms of shock to the fake pill, rather than to the shock, and would thus be willing to tolerate more shock than people not given the pill. Indeed, the effect was enormous—people given the fake pill took four times as much shock. Afterwards, informed they had taken more shock than average, they were asked why. Not only did their answers make no reference to the pill, when pressed, and even after the experimenter explained the hypotheses of the experiment in detail, they denied any influence of the pill. They would usually say the pill likely did affect *others*, but not themselves; "I didn't even think about the pill" was a typical reply.

Many other experiments make evident a similar lack of self-insight. For example, although it has been shown that a bystander is usually much less willing to help a person in distress when several others are present, the participants in these experiments usually denied that the others' presence influenced them in the slightest. Experiments have also found that people give more positive ratings to another person if they expected to meet that person; yet they deny they have done so—"I wasn't affected by the fact I was going to meet her. How could that possibly affect what I thought about her?"

Not only are we often unaware of what has influenced our behavior, but we then also frequently explain our actions in grossly incorrect ways. Nisbett and Timothy Wilson had people watch a videotaped interview of a man who, in one version of the tape, responded warmly and, in another, coldly. The viewers then rated not only their liking for the man, but also a number of other traits, including his physical attractiveness, French accent, etc. Those who saw the "cold" interview rated most of his traits very negatively, while those who saw the "warm" interview rated most of his traits positively. But interviewed afterwards, the subjects denied that their overall liking of the man had any influence upon their ratings of specific traits; instead they insisted that their evaluations of his traits had been responsible for their liking or disliking him. But on the two videotapes the man's traits (physical appearance, accent, etc.) were identical. Clearly, the subjects' convictions, though sincere, were grossly erroneous. Their perception of the cause-effect sequence was the *opposite* of what really occurred: their liking or disliking of the man had determined their ratings of his traits, not the other way around as they thought.

Finally, we often poorly predict our own future behavior. When asked whether they would accede to demands to deliver cruel electric shocks, or would be hesitant to help a victim if several other people were present, people overwhelmingly deny their vulnerability to such influences. But experiments have shown that many of us are vulnerable.

To a striking extent, then, we often make false assertions about what we have done, why we did such, and what we will do. However, we must be careful not to overstate the matter. When the causes of behavior are conspicuous and the correct explanation fits our intuition, our self-perceptions can be accurate. It is when the causes of behavior are not obvious that our self-explanations become more erroneous.

How little we actualize Thales' advice to "Know thyself" is also reinforced by cognitive psychologists, who contend that we are unaware of much that goes on in our minds.[8] Studies of perception and memory show that our awareness is mostly of the *results* of our thinking and not of the process of our thinking. For example, asked where the letter "r" is on the keyboard, a typist will have difficulty answering verbally; the knowledge is, so to speak, "in the fingers."[9] Ernest Hilgard's recent book, *Divided Consciousness*, is replete with many more astounding examples of the extent to which we think—register and process information, construct memories, etc.—without being aware we are doing so.[10] Drawing upon data ranging from classic reports of possession states and multiple personalities to rigorous modern experiments, Hilgard drives home the conclusion that conscious awareness is but one subsystem in a marvelously complex and intricate system for processing information. For example, his own hypnosis experiments demonstrate that hypnotized people have a "hidden observer" that can receive information and write answers to questions even while the person is consciously discussing an unrelated topic. In less dramatic ways, we all have experienced the results of our mind's unconscious workings—when we set an unconscious mental clock to record the passage of time and to awaken us at an appointed hour, or when we achieve a seemingly spontaneous creative insight after a problem has unconsciously "incubated."

This research on the imperfections of our self-knowledge has at least two implications. The first is for psychological inquiry. The introspections of one's clients or research subjects may provide some useful clues to their psychological processes, but these self-reports are not trustworthy explanations. People's errors in self-understanding place limits on the usefulness of their subjective personal reports.[11]

The second implication has ramifications for everyday life. The sincerity with which people give witness to and interpret their experiences is no guarantee of the validity of these personal reports. As we shall later note, personal testimonies are powerfully persuasive. However, they are fraught with the potential for unwitting error. Our failure to recognize the extent of potential error renders us gullible to believing all sorts of false proclamations.

OUR BELIEFS CONTROL OUR INTERPRETATIONS AND MEMORIES

The human mind resembles those uneven mirrors which impart their own properties to different objects . . . The human understanding, when any proposition has been once laid down (either from general admission and belief, or from the pleasure it affords), forces everything else to add fresh support and confirmation.[12]

FRANCIS BACON

In every arena of human thinking our prior beliefs bias our perceptions, interpretations, and memories. Most of us do not need experiments to acknowledge this. Yet generally we fail to realize the impact of our prejudgments. Our tendency to perceive events in terms of our beliefs is one of the most significant facts concerning the workings of our minds.

Evidence for this truth is standard fare for introductory courses in psychology. Numerous demonstrations illustrate that what students will see in a picture can be influenced by what they are led to expect. More recent evidence suggests that our prior expectations also have an enormous effect upon our perception of relationships among events in the world. For example, Stanford researchers Dennis Jennings and Lee Ross found that when people were shown data indicating a definite relationship between two things which they did not connect in their minds, they grossly underestimated the magnitude of the relationship. But when asked to estimate the relationship between two things which they believed to be related (e.g., between a child's honesty in one situation and the child's honesty in a second situation), they perceived a much closer relationship than really existed.[13] This suggests that our beliefs about the social world are frequently influenced more by our theories and expectations than by observable facts. Our processing of information is "theory driven."

David Halberstam recounts an anecdote from the Vietnam War which illustrates the phenomenon. General Westmoreland was about to be informed of the incompetence of South Vietnamese soldiers:

> Westmoreland had demanded the briefing and the young American had been uneasy about giving it, apologizing for being so frank with a reporter present, but finally it had come pouring out: the ARVN soldiers were cowards, they refused to fight, they abused the population, in their most recent battle they had all fled, all but one man. That one man had stood and fought and almost single-handedly staved off a Vietcong attack. When the officer had finished his briefing, still apologizing for being so candid, Westmoreland turned to McGinnis and said: "Now you see how distorted the press image of this war is. This is a perfect example—a great act of bravery and not a single mention of it in *The New York Times*."[14]

People's prejudgments make it difficult for them to perceive the evil in which they are enmeshed. Lewis Coser has observed that after World War II the "good people" of Germany typically denied that they had been conscious of or had participated in evildoing.[15] Evil is invisible, Coser surmised, until its visibility becomes publicly sanctioned. Recently, in an old children's reader, I saw Jane sprawled on the sidewalk, her roller skates beside her, as Mark explained to his mother:

> "She can not skate," said Mark.
> "I can help her.
> I want to help her.
> Look at her, mother.

Just look at her.
She's just like a girl.
She gives up."

When did the sexism of such narratives become visible? Not until the 1970s did its visibility become public, not until our new beliefs about the sexes fostered new perceptions of such portrayals.

This tendency to prejudge reality on the basis of our beliefs has implications for science.[16] Most behavioral scientists underestimate the extent to which beliefs and values penetrate science. Philosophers of science have therefore been reminding us that our observations of reality are always "theory-laden." There is an objective reality out there, but we are always viewing it through the spectacles of our preconceived beliefs and values. Scientists—and lay people—don't merely read what's out there in the book of nature; rather, they squeeze nature into their own mental categories. The reactions of various scientists to claims about the Shroud of Turin, which some believe to be the cloth in which Jesus' body was wrapped, reveal nearly as much about the scientists' underlying beliefs as they do about the Shroud.[17] Likewise, the conclusions I have drawn from the experiments described in this book are simply my conclusions, not something that nature handed me on tablets of stone.

The impact of our assumptions is similarly evident in theology and in biblical interpretation. Our prior beliefs influence the questions we bring to the Bible and the answers we elicit from it. Feminism is a current example: those for and against it both find the Bible supporting their position. It almost seems as if people are reasoning:

Feminism is right (wrong).
The Bible teaches what is right.
Therefore the Bible teaches (does not teach) feminism.

As Jack Rogers put it, "The faith with which one begins radically determines the interpretation that will be given the data examined."[18] Karl Barth reached the same conclusion: "When the Word of God meets us, we are laden with the images, ideas and certainties which we ourselves have formed about God, the world and ourselves. In the fog of this intellectual life of ours the Word of God, which is clear in itself, always becomes obscure."[19] We are never in an intellectual vacuum, thinking free of the control of prior thought. Our basic belief system is therefore very important, for it shapes our interpretation of everything else.

Charles Lord and his Stanford University colleagues have documented the incredible biasing power of our beliefs. They showed college students, half of whom favored and half of whom opposed capital punishment, two purported new research studies. One study confirmed and the other disconfirmed the students' existing beliefs about the crime-deterring effectiveness of the death penalty. Both the proponents and opponents of capital punishment readily accepted the evidence which confirmed their belief, but were sharply critical of the "disconfirming" evidence. Showing the two sides an identical body of mixed evidence had therefore not narrowed their disagreement, but increased it. Each side had perceived the evidence as supporting its belief and now believed even more strongly.[20]

That presuppositions affect scientific, religious, and every-day thinking is becoming an accepted fact. Less well known are some recent experiments which systematically manipulate people's presuppositions, with astonishing effects upon how they interpret and recall what they observe. Melvin Snyder and Arthur Frankel showed people a silent videotape of a woman being interviewed.[21] Those told she was being interviewed about sex perceived her as more anxious during the interview and as a generally more anxious person than did those who were told she was being interviewed about politics.

Other experiments have planted a falsehood in people's minds and then tried to discredit it. As Lee Ross and his colleagues demonstrated in an ingenious series of experiments, it can be surprisingly difficult to demolish a falsehood, once the person has conjured up a rationale for it. In each experiment, first a belief was established, either by proclaiming it true or else by inducing the person to conclude its truth after inspecting two sample cases; then, people were asked to explain *why* it was true; and, finally, the initial information was totally discredited—the person was told the truth, that the information was manufactured for the experiment and that half the people in the experiment were given opposing theory or data. Nevertheless, amazingly, the new belief typically survived the discrediting about 75% intact, presumably because the person still retained the invented explanation for the belief.

For instance, Craig Anderson and Ross asked people to decide whether people who take risks make good or bad firefighters.[22] They were given only two concrete cases to inspect; one group was shown a risky person being a susccessful firefighter and a cautious person an unsuccessful one. The other group was shown cases suggesting the opposite conclusion. After forming their theory that risky people make better or worse firefighters, the people wrote an explanation for it. Those who were induced to believe in the superiority of risky people typically reasoned that being quick to take a risk is conducive to bravery in saving occupants from a burning building. Those who theorized the reverse explained that successful firefighters are careful, unimpulsive people who are not likely to risk their own and others' lives. Once formed, each explanation could exist independent of the information which initially created the belief. Thus when that information was discredited, the people still held their self-generated explanations and therefore continued to believe that risky people really *do* make better or worse firefighters.

These experiments go on to indicate that, paradoxically, the more closely we examine our theories and understand and explain how they *might* be true, the more closed we become to cogent discrediting information. And there is every reason to think the phenomenon is true of scientists and clinicians, too. Scientific theories sometimes are amazingly resilient to disconfirming evidence. You may also wish to ponder the implications of this for religion. What are the consequences of inventing a religious doctrine (or, for that matter, an antireligious doctrine) and then explaining and defending its plausibility?

Our beliefs, even if false, are perpetuated in additional ways. People routinely oversimplify the explanation of complex events. Harriet Shaklee and Baruch Fischhoff have found that once people identify a cause which seems to help explain an event, other contributing causes are discounted.[23] This phenomenon surely occurs in everyday experience. For instance, the background of a juvenile delinquent may differ in so many ways from that of the average nondelinquent that nearly any simplistic theory of delinquency can be "verified" by casual observation, thus allowing one to discount other competing explanations. Moreover, we are inclined to "assimilate" events—to interpret and recall them in ways compatible with what we already believe. Thus we much more readily incorporate a new fact within our beliefs than revise our beliefs in light of the fact,[24] and we best remember information when it is consistent with our ideas.[25]

Erroneous beliefs are also sustained by another potent phenomenon. First, consider whether you agree or disagree with this statement:

> Memory can be likened to a storage chest in the brain into which we deposit material and from which we can withdraw it later if needed.

> Occasionally, something gets lost from the "chest," and then we say
> we have forgotten.

About 85% of college students agree with this statement.[26]
But it is false. Our memories are not copies of our past
experience which remain on deposit. Rather, they are
reconstructed at the time of withdrawal. Like a paleontologist
inferring the appearance of a dinosaur from bone fragments,
we reconstruct our distant past from fragments of information. You can demonstrate this by recalling a scene from a
pleasurable past experience. Do you see yourself in the
scene? If so, your memory must be a reconstruction of what
you experienced, for we do not in reality look at ourselves.
Since people are mostly unaware of the errors and distortions
which they build into the reconstruction, they will often
be sure enough of their false beliefs to stake money on them.
According to one poll, 70% of Americans remember seeing
the assassination of John F. Kennedy on television in 1963.
The truth is that although still photos were published in
magazines, the film was not shown on television until 1976.[27]

Studies of conflicting eyewitness testimonies further illustrate our tendency to recall the past with great confidence but
meager accuracy. Elizabeth Loftus and John Palmer showed
people a film of a traffic accident and then asked them
questions about what they saw.[28] People who were asked
"How fast were the cars going when they smashed into each
other?" gave higher estimates than those asked "How fast
were the cars going when they hit each other?" A week later
they were also asked whether they recalled seeing any broken
glass. Although there was no broken glass in the accident,
people asked the question with "smashed" were more than
twice as likely as those asked the question with "hit" to report
seeing broken glass. This demonstrates how in constructing a
memory we unconsciously use our general knowledge and
beliefs to fill in the holes, thus organizing mere fragments
from our actual past into a convincing memory.

A recent experiment by Mark Snyder and Seymour Uranowitz shows the extent to which our beliefs shape our memories.[25] They had their University of Minnesota students read identical descriptions of the life of a woman named Betty K. Later, they told some that Betty was now a lesbian; they informed others that she was heterosexual. They then asked the students to recall events from Betty's life. (If by now I have convinced you of the extent to which our beliefs bias our memories, you should have no difficulty predicting the result.) The people who were told that Betty was lesbian reconstructed the events of her life in a manner reflecting stereotyped beliefs about lesbians, and likewise for those told she was heterosexual.

As we shall see later, psychiatrists and clinical psychologists are not immune to these powerful, unwitting human tendencies. *We all selectively notice, perceive, interpret, and recall events in ways which sustain our ideas.* Such are the gymnastics which our minds perform to perpetuate our beliefs.

CHAPTER 5

How We Form and Sustain False Beliefs: II

We have seen how easily we can form false impressions of what we've done, why we did it, what we've been thinking, and what we will do. And we have seen how our beliefs bias our perceptions, interpretations, and memories. Our tendency to reconstruct our memories in terms of what we currently believe provides the foundation for yet another illusion of human thought: overestimating, after an event has occurred, our ability to have predicted it beforehand.

THE I-KNEW-IT-ALL-ALONG PHENOMENON

Events are far more "obvious" and predictable in hindsight than beforehand. Baruch Fischhoff and his colleagues have demonstrated that once we know what really did happen, we instantly distort our recollection of what outcomes we would have expected from some experiment or historical situation.[1] In one of Fischhoff's experiments, Israeli students estimated the likelihood of possible outcomes of President Nixon's forthcoming trips to Peking and Moscow.[2] When, after his visits, the students were asked unexpectedly to remember their predictions, they misremembered them as coinciding closely with what they now knew had happened. Finding out that something had happened made it seem more inevitable. Likewise, in everyday life we often do not expect something to happen. But when it does, we then suddenly see clearly the forces which brought it to be and thus seldom feel surprised.

We say we "really knew all along" such was going to occur.

If the I-knew-it-all-along phenomenon is pervasive, you may be feeling now that you "knew it all along." Almost any result of a psychological experiment can seem like common sense—*after* you know the result. Try this out on some friends. Give half of them some purported psychological finding and give the other half the opposite result. Ask each group to explain the result. Then ask whether it seems surprising or not surprising. Make up your own or try these:

> Social psychologists have found that whether choosing friends or falling in love, we are most attracted to people whose traits are different from our own. There seems to be wisdom in the old saying that "opposites attract."

> Social psychologists have found that whether choosing friends or falling in love, we are most attracted to people whose traits are similar to our own. There seems to be wisdom in the old saying that "birds of a feather flock together."

As these examples indicate, we can draw upon a stockpile of proverbs to make almost any result seem commonsensical. If a psychologist finds that separation intensifies romantic attraction, someone is sure to reply "Of course, 'Absence makes the heart grow fonder.'" Should the result be the reverse, the same person may remind us that "Out of sight, out of mind."

This hindsight bias creates a problem for many psychology students. When they read the results of experiments in their textbooks the material often seems easy, even commonsensical. When they subsequently take a multiple-choice test on which they must choose among several plausible outcomes to an experiment, they may find that task surprisingly difficult. "I don't know what happened," the befuddled student later bemoans. "I thought I knew the material."

The I-knew-it-all-along phenomenon also affects our assessments of the extent of our past knowledge. If what we learn does not surprise us, then we are inclined to overestimate how much we already knew. Consider this question, to which *a* is the answer: "Is absinthe a) a liquor or b) a precious stone?" When Fischhoff asked University of Oregon students to estimate the likelihood they could have answered such questions if he hadn't told them the answers, they indicated more certainty than did students not told the answers.

Since you and I know about the phenomenon we will not be as vulnerable to it as the Oregon students, will we? Fischhoff wondered about this, also. He forewarned some more Oregon students that on such questions people

> exaggerate how much they have known without being told the answer. You might call this an I-knew-it-all-along effect . . . A group of people who were told the correct answer was *a* believed that they would have assigned a probability of about .60 to *a*. A group of people who were not told the answer believed the item was a toss-up. They assigned a probability of .50 to *a*. In completing the present questionnaire, please do everything you can to avoid this bias. One reason why it happens is that people who are told the correct answer find it hard to imagine how they ever could have believed in the incorrect one. In answering, make certain that you haven't forgotten any reasons that you might have thought of in favor of the wrong answer—had you not been told it was wrong.[3]

Do you think these "debiasing instructions" had much effect? Incredible as it sounds, they had no effect. Being fully forewarned about the hindsight bias reduces it not at all! (Surely, though, now that you and I know the result of *this* experiment. . . .)

Our intellectual conceit can have pernicious personal and social consequences. We can arrogantly overestimate our own intellectual powers and the perceptiveness of our after-the-fact explanations. We are also more likely to blame decision-makers for what are, in retrospect, their "obvious" bad choices than we are to praise them for their good choices, since these, too, were "obvious." Thus, *after* the Japanese attacked Pearl Harbor, Monday morning historians could read the signs and see the "inevitability" of what had happened.

Likewise, we sometimes chastise ourselves for our "stupid mistakes"—for not having better handled a situation or a person, for example. Although we are usually more understanding of our own mistakes than of others' mistakes, we may nevertheless be too hard on ourselves as well. We may forget that what is now obvious to us was not nearly so obvious at the time.

WE OVERESTIMATE THE ACCURACY OF OUR JUDGMENTS

The intellectual conceit, evident in our judgments of our past knowledge (the I-knew-it-all-along phenomenon), extends to estimates of our current knowledge. For example, Amos Tversky and Daniel Kahneman gave people almanac-type questions, similar to this:[4]

> How many foreign cars were imported into the U.S. in 1979?
>
> (a) Make a high estimate such that you feel there is only a 1% probability the true answer would exceed your estimate.
>
> (b) Make a low estimate such that you feel there is only a 1% probability the true answer would be below this estimate.

Thus people were asked to estimate a range of figures broad enough to make it 98% certain that the true answer (2,284, 500, for this question) would be within that range. But the people apparently failed to appreciate the extent to which errors would creep into their reasoning: Nearly 50% of the time, the true answer to the questions lay outside the range in which people were 98% confident. When Fischhoff and his associates asked people to indicate their certainty while answering factual multiple-choice questions, the same over-confidence phenomenon occurred. The probability of the people's choosing the right answer was typically much less than what they felt the probability to be.[5] This finding has now been observed in several experiments; if people say the chances are 70% that their answer to a factual question is right, the odds are about 50-50 that they will be wrong.

Overconfidence is an accepted fact in experimental psychology. The issue now is what produces it. Why, given our fallibility, are we so confident of our judgments? Why does experience not lead us to a more realistic self-appraisal? There are a number of reasons.[6] For one thing, people are not inclined to seek out information that might disprove what they believe. P. C. Wason demonstrated this, as you can, by giving people a sequence of three numbers, such as 2, 4, 6, which conformed to a rule he had in mind (the rule was simply three ascending numbers).[7] To enable the people to discover the rule, Wason allowed each person to generate sets of three numbers. Each time Wason told the person whether the set did or didn't conform to the rule. When sure they had discovered the rule, the people were to stop and announce it. The result? Seldom right, but never in doubt: 23 out of 29 people convinced themselves of a wrong rule. They had formed some erroneous belief as to what Wason's rule was (e.g., counting by twos) and then searched for only *confirming* evidence rather than attempt to *disconfirm* their hunches. Other experiments also indicate that *it is hard for us to discard our ideas.* We are eager to verify our beliefs, but we are not inclined to seek evidence which might disprove our beliefs.

With this forewarning, see how you do on this question, adapted from another of Wason's experiments.[8] Pretend I were to show you four cards, each with a letter on one side and a number on the other. The sides facing up show D, 3, B, 7. What cards would you need to turn over to test this rule?: "If there is a D on one side of any card, there is a 3 on the other side."

You probably first chose to turn over the D to try to verify the rule. That's okay. What other card would you choose? Wason's subjects chose the 3—again trying to *verify* the rule.

But if the 3 had some other letter, that wouldn't disprove the rule. The correct second choice is 7, which, if it had a D on the other side, *would* disprove the rule.

In everyday life, what *happens* more readily catches our attention than what *doesn't* happen. For example, most people do reasonably well at their jobs. Therefore, managers may feel confident of their ability to identify promising applicants; as they scan their employees, they are gratified by how well most are doing. The managers cannot examine those they passed up, so it is difficult to imagine how managers could disconfirm any overconfidence in their hiring ability. [9]

Editors' assessments of manuscripts also reveal the extent of error in human judgment. In psychology, for example, studies have revealed that there is usually a distressingly modest relationship between one reviewer's evaluation of a manuscript and a second reviewer's evaluation. It's not just true of psychology. Writer Chuck Ross, using a pseudonym, mailed a typewritten copy of Jerzy Kosinski's novel *Steps* to 28 major publishers and literary agencies. All rejected it, including Random House, which published the book in 1968 and watched it win the National Book Award and sell more than 400,000 copies. [10]

THE PERSUASIVE POWER OF ANECDOTES

A panel of psychologists interviewed a sample of 30 engineers and 70 lawyers, and summarized their impressions in thumbnail descriptions of those individuals. The following description has been drawn at random from the sample of 30 engineers and 70 lawyers.

Jack is a 39-year-old man. He is married and has two children. He is active in local politics. The hobby that he most enjoys is rare book collection. He is competitive, argumentative, and articulate. Question: What is the probability that Jack is a lawyer rather than an engineer?

When Daniel Kahneman and Amos Tversky presented this question to University of Oregon students, most answered

95% or better.[11] Switching the population information to indicate that 70% of the people in the group were *engineers* had little effect on the answers. Most students still said that the chances are 95% or better that Jack is a lawyer. This result, and many others like it, illustrates the extent to which we rely upon concrete information and ignore reliable, but abstract, information. Such is true even when the anecdotal description is acknowledged by everyone—experimenters and subjects alike—to be of dubious validity (e.g., when it is known to have come from an unreliable test).

Given no information about Jack, people will correctly say that the chances of his being a lawyer are 70%, if that is the frequency of lawyers in the population. But what will they do if given worthless information about Jack—will they ignore it and still say the odds of his being a lawyer are 70%? Read someone the above paragraph about 30 engineers and 70 lawyers and then ask this question:

> Jack is a 39-year-old man. He is married, with no children. A man of high ability and high motivation, he promises to be quite successful in his field. He is well liked by his colleagues. Question: What is the probability that Jack is a lawyer rather than an engineer?

Most people recognize that this information contains no clues to whether Jack is a lawyer or engineer, for they typically say that it's 50-50 which he is—*regardless* of whether they were told his group was 70% lawyers or 30% lawyers.[12] Giving people even obviously useless information often prompts them to ignore useful information about population frequency.

Our willingness to ignore useful information and use useless information is also apparent in some amusing new experiments. The following two questions are adapted from an experiment by Henry Zukier of the New School for Social Research.[13]

Roberta is a university student who spends about 3 hours studying outside of classes in an average week. What would you guess her grade point average to be?

Judith is a university student who spends about 3 hours studying outside of classes in an average week. Judith has four plants in the place she's living in now. On an average weekday, she goes to sleep around midnight. She has a brother and two sisters. Two months was the longest she dated one person. She describes herself as often being a cheerful person. What would you guess her grade point average to be?

The first question has but one bit of useful information. Those given it usually estimated low grades. People given questions such as the second—with worthless bits of information—did not believe there is any connection between how many plants one has and grade average. Yet, when such information was added to the useful information about study time, it diluted the impact of the useful information—so much so that it no longer made much difference whether the hypothetical student was said to study 3 or 31 hours per week!

Harvard psychologist Ellen Langer and her colleagues have also demonstrated our use of useless information.[14] For example, they made a simple request of people about to use a copying machine. Forty percent of those approached with "Excuse me, I have five pages. May I use the Xerox machine?" declined the request. But only 7% refused when the request was accompanied by a nonsensical justification: "Excuse me, I have five pages. May I use the Xerox machine, because I have to make copies."

Researchers Richard Nisbett and Eugene Borgida, exploring the tendency to overuse anecdotal information, showed people videotaped interviews of other people who were supposedly subjects in an experiment that elicited inhumane acts from most of its subjects.[15] Being told how most subjects really acted had almost no effect upon people's predictions of how the individual they observed acted. The apparent niceness of this individual was more vivid and compelling than the general truth about how most people really acted: "Ted seems so pleasant that I can't imagine him being unresponsive to another's plight." Their focusing upon the specific individual seemed to push into the background useful information about the population the person came from. There is, of course, a positive side to viewing other individuals as individuals and not merely as statistical units. But a problem arises when we formulate our beliefs about people in general from our observations of particular persons; preoccupation with individuals can easily distort our perception of what is generally true. Our impressions of a group, for example, tend to be overly influenced by extreme members of the group.

More than 50 years ago Betrand Russell proposed that "popular induction depends upon the emotional interest of the instances, not upon their numbers."[16] The principle can now be restated based on recent research: People are slow to deduce particular instances from a general truth, but are remarkably quick to infer general truth from a vivid instance. One University of Michigan study found that a single vivid welfare case had more effect on people's opinions about welfare recipients than did factual statistics about welfare cases. Similarly, all physicians know about the statistical connection between smoking and cancer. But it's radiologists and others who have seen the connection most vividly that are the least likely to smoke.

Or ponder this finding: student impressions of potential teachers have been found to be influenced more by a few personal testimonies concerning the teacher than by a comprehensive statistical summary of many students' evaluations. A single face-to-face testimony should simply increase the statistical summary by one more person. But, in reality, one or two testimonials may have more impact than the statistically summarized testimonials of hundreds of people. Thus the mastectomies performed on Betty Ford and Happy Rockefeller did more to increase visits to cancer detection clinics than all the reports of the National Institutes of Health. And a few highly vivid instances of political wrongdoing have substantially depressed Americans' faith in politicians.

People's individual testimonies are more compelling than general information partly because vivid information is more easily brought to mind; it claims a disproportionate share of our attention.

Question: Does the letter k appear more often as the first letter of a word or as the third letter?

Answer: The letter k is three times more likely to appear as the third letter of an English word than as the first. Yet, most people judge that k appears more often at the beginning of a word. We can more easily recall words beginning with k, Kahneman and Tversky surmise, and ease of recall is our basis for judging the frequency of events.

Likewise, the perceived frequency of car accidents rises more if we see an accident (a vivid event) than if we only read about the accident.

Question: What percent of deaths in the U.S. each year are due to:
_____accidents
_____cardiovascular diseases?

Answer: Cardiovascular diseases cause ten times as many deaths as accidents: 50% vs. 5%. Most people overestimate the frequency of accidents, which are more vivid and memorable.

It is a sad fact, but when information from a vivid incident is available, most people disregard rationally compelling data.[17] Our predisposition to be easily persuaded by striking testimonials, by anecdotes of changed lives, and by our own intuitive judgments based on limited information has profound implications for everyday life. Thus state lotteries, which return less than half of the billions of dollars they take in, exploit the impact of a few winners. Because the statistical reality always stays buried in the back of people's minds, the lottery system seduces people into perceiving a lottery ticket as having a much greater earnings potential than it actually does.

The impact of a vivid anecdote is well known to effective speakers and writers. A vivid image can bring to life the general truth that it illustrates. As William Strunk and E. B. White assert in their classic, *The Elements of Style*,

> If those who have studied the art of writing are in accord on any one point, it is on this: the surest way to arouse and hold the attention of the reader is by being specific, definite, and concrete. The greatest writers—Homer, Dante, Shakespeare—are effective largely because they deal in particular particulars. . . . [18]

The Hebrew language draws power from its rich use of visual images. Teachers have learned by experience that engaging everyday examples of basic principles help students grasp the principles. (In fact, one experiment found that students remembered extraneous jokes and announcements embedded in classroom lectures better than they remembered the lectures. [19]) Vivid instances and testimonials have a rich, compelling quality—but sometimes so rich and compelling that we are persuaded even when those instances are grossly unrepresentative of human experience. As an old Yiddish saying reminds us: "For example is no proof."

We can summarize the persuasive power of anecdotes by noting that another of Francis Bacon's verdicts has been empirically confirmed:

> The human understanding is most excited by that which strikes and enters the mind at once and suddenly, and by which the imagination is immediately filled and inflated. It then begins almost imperceptibly to conceive and suppose that everything is similar to the few objects which have taken possession of the mind, whilst it is very slow and unfit for the transition to the remote and heterogeneous instances by which axioms are tried as by fire. [20]

CHAPTER 6

How We Form and
Sustain False Beliefs: III

Self-deceptions, powerful biases, intellectual conceit, and difficulties in discerning general truth all help create the illusions of human thought. And still there is more.

ILLUSIONS OF CAUSATION, CORRELATION, AND PERSONAL CONTROL

Our vulnerability to false beliefs is further increased by three more illusions of human thought. Having in a previous book described in some detail these interrelated illusions, I shall but summarize them here.[1]

Correlation and Causation

The one mistake of human thinking known by nearly every student of psychology is the nearly irresistible temptation to assume that two events that occur together are necessarily causally connected. To be sure, there is a relationship between people's educational attainments and their earnings, between certain child-rearing styles and the personalities of those children thus brought up, and between health practices and longevity. But, having discerned these relationships, we too readily jump to the conclusion that education pays financial dividends, that specific child-rearing styles have predictable effects, and that life expectancy can be manipulated by changes in nutrition and exercise. Each conclusion may be true, but none is established by the mere correlation within each pair. The association in each case has other plausible explanations. With a bit of logic you can provide them. For example, granted parenting technique is associated with the characteristics of the child, but might this not also be because of their shared heredity or because the child's personality elicits specific reactions from the parents?

Sometimes a coincidental association between two events induces a fallacious conviction that one causes the other. Experiments with animals, children, and adults demonstrate that the power of coincidence can produce superstitious behaviors. If an act such as a good luck ritual just happens to be performed before the occurrence of a rewarding event, one could easily assume that the act *caused* the reward. Such a presumption can incline an animal or person to perform that act ever more frequently, and thus increase the probability that the act will be performed shortly before the reward comes. (This is part of the magic of experimental psychology —pulling habits out of a rat.) Of course, only very occasionally will a reward, indeed, follow the behavior. But this erratic "intermittent reinforcement," as experimental psychologists call it, is especially conducive to persistent behavior. If a hungry pigeon is given a food pellet every so often regardless of what it is doing, the pigeon will often develop some ritualistic behavior and, after the pellets are discontinued, perform that act 10,000 times or more before quitting.[2] It's as if the pigeon believes that, in the past, its patient persistence was eventually rewarded.

The phenomenon occurs often in everyday life. Near Seattle, on the island where I grew up, we all had our "lucky fishing spots"—where we once caught a good-sized salmon. There we continued fishing, eventually catching more. George Gmelch has described the superstitious behaviors of baseball pitchers and hitters.[3] Pitching and hitting involve considerable chance and uncertainty and thus are much more vulnerable to the development of personal rituals than is fielding, where the player's personal control is much higher and the success rate is already near perfection (.975 on the average).

The power of coincidence is also evident in acts undertaken to ward off tragedy. If, for instance, a tragedy does not occur while one wears a rabbit's foot, then the "success" of that ritual may prompt its continuation. Some of these behaviors may have at one time actually enabled people to avoid some fearful events and thus may have lasted because the fear is reduced when they continue to avoid what frightens them.

Illusory Correlation

Our confusion concerning correlation-causation is often compounded by our susceptibility to perceiving correlation where none exists. When we expect to see significant relationships, we easily misperceive random events as significantly related. In one experiment, people were shown the results of a hypothetical cloud seeding experiment. Each day for 50 days the clouds supposedly had either been seeded or not and it rained or did not. Shown a random mix of results (regardless of whether the clouds were seeded, it sometimes rained and sometimes not), the people nevertheless were convinced—in conformity with their intuitive supposition about the effects of cloud seeding—that they really had observed a relationship between cloud seeding and rain.[4]

This and other similar experiments indicate that people easily misperceive random events as confirming their beliefs. When we believe a correlation exists between two things, we are more likely to notice and recall confirming than disconfirming instances. The joint occurrence of two unusual events—say the premonition of a strange event and the subsequent occurrence of that event—is especially likely to be noticed and remembered, far more than all the times those unusual events do not coincide. Hence, we easily overestimate the frequency with which these strange things happen.

If, after thinking about a friend, that friend calls us, we are far more likely to notice and remember this coincidence than all the times we think of a friend without any ensuing call, or receive a call from a friend about whom we have not been thinking.

The difficulty we have recognizing coincidental, random events for what they are predisposes us to perceive order even when shown a purely random series of events. Try this question: If someone were to flip a coin six times, would one of these sequences of heads (H) and tails (T) be more likely than the other two: HHHTTT or HTTHTH or HHHHHH? Kahneman and Tversky have found that HTTHTH and its mirror image seem more random to people than all other possible sequences.[5] Actually, all the possible sequences are equally likely. Bridge players would find it extraordinary if they were dealt a hand with all cards of one suit. In reality, this is no more unlikely than any other hand they might be dealt. A mathematician friend of mine recently constructed a wall of red, white, and black bricks by placing the bricks with the aid of a table of random numbers. As chance would have it, the resulting wall did not *look* random, because it had one large area with no black bricks. To make the pattern visually appear random, she therefore violated her random assignment plan and moved one black brick to the center of this area. Such is our disinclination to recognize chance occurrences for what they are.[6]

Illusion of Control

Our tending to perceive random events as though they were related feeds the frequent illusion that chance events are subject to our personal control. Ellen Langer has demonstrated this with experiments on gambling behavior.[7] People were easily seduced into believing they could beat chance. If they chose a lottery number for themselves they demanded four times as much money for the sale of their lottery ticket as people whose number was assigned by the experimenter. If they played a game of chance against an awkward and nervous person, they were willing to bet significantly more than when playing against a dapper, confident opponent. In these and other ways Langer consistently observed that people act as if they can control chance events—especially when they succeed at first. Apparently, early success entices people to perceive themselves as skilled and, as noted in the research on illusory correlation, they then will be likely to misperceive subsequent events as confirming their belief. If, in what are obviously chance situations, we are vulnerable to an illusion of personal control, we are likely even more vulnerable in situations that combine chance and skill, such as when pitching or hitting.

Let's imagine a study. Some students who scored very low on the Medical College Admissions Test sign up for a course on how to score high on the test. After the course they retake the test, and most of them score higher. Does this indicate that the course was beneficial, at least for these students?

No, this finding could reflect the phenomenon of "regression toward the average," which often contributes to the illusion of control. For example, people who score extremely high or low on a test are more likely, when retested, to fall back ("regress") toward the middle than to become even more extreme: when you are at the very bottom the only direction you can move is up. Thus the average student who scored surprisingly low on the medical school aptitude examination will likely score slightly higher the next time, leading the student to believe in the usefulness of the course even if it had no effect. When things are desperately bad we will try anything rather than sit passively, and whatever we try—going to a psychotherapist, starting a new diet/exercise plan, reading a self-help book—is more likely to be followed by improvement than by further decrement. Thus it seems effective, even if the activity had no effect.

Sometimes we do recognize that events can seldom continue at an unusually good or bad extreme. Experience has taught us that when everything is going great, something will go wrong, and that when life is dealing us terrible blows we can usually look forward to things getting better. Often, though, we fail to recognize this regression effect. When the accomplishments of a Nobel Prize-winning scientist diminish after his winning the prize, or when a baseball player's hitting streak ends, these are instances of achievement falling back to more normal levels. But it is nevertheless tempting to invent special theories to explain these regressions. For example, a football coach who rewards his team with lavish praise and a light practice after their best game of the season and harasses them after an exceptionally bad game may soon conclude that rewards lead to poorer performance in the next game while punishments improve performance. Parents and teachers may reach the same conclusion after reacting to extremely good or bad behaviors. Thus nature operates in such a way that we are often punished for rewarding others and rewarded for punishing others.

ERRONEOUS BELIEFS MAY GENERATE THEIR OWN REALITY

One additional reason why false beliefs are so resistant to disconfirmation is that our beliefs sometimes lead us to act in ways which elicit an apparent confirmation of our beliefs. It is, for example, well known that children often live up to what's expected of them. The famous studies of experimenter bias and teacher expectations indicate that at least sometimes (these effects are not as reliable as commonly thought), the erroneous belief that certain people are unusually capable (or incapable) can lead one to give special treatment to those people. This may elicit superior (or inferior) performance, and therefore seem to confirm an assumption that is actually false.

In laboratory games, hostility nearly always begets hostility: people who perceive their opponents as hostile will readily induce them to *be* hostile.[8] Self-confirming beliefs abound in times of conflict. Each party's perception of the other as attacking, resentful, and vindictive induces the other to display these behaviors in self-defense, thus creating a vicious self-perpetuating circle. For example, married persons may act in ways that induce each other to confirm their perception of the spouse's hostile feelings.

Several experiments by Mark Snyder of the University of Minnesota show how, once formed, erroneous beliefs about the social world can induce others to confirm those beliefs. In one study, men students had a phone conversation with women they thought (from having been shown a picture) were either attractive or unattractive.[9] Analysis of just the women's comments during the conversations revealed that the women who were presumed attractive were in fact more likable and warmer than the women who were presumed unattractive. The men's erroneous beliefs had become a self-fulfilling prophecy, leading them to act in a way that influenced the women to fulfill their stereotype that beautiful people are good people. In another experiment, Snyder and William Swann found that when people interacted with someone who expected them to be hostile, they were indeed hostile. When conditions led them to see this hostility as a reflection of themselves, they subsequently were also more hostile to a naive person who had no prior knowledge about them.[10] These experiments help us understand how social beliefs, such as stereotypes about handicapped people or about people of a particular race or sex, may be self-confirming. We help construct our own social realities. How others treat us reflects how we and others have treated them. Thus whether I expect my wife to be in a bad mood or in a warm, loving mood may affect how I relate to her, thereby inducing her to confirm my belief.

OTHER FOIBLES OF HUMAN THINKING

Many other research findings testify to the magnitude of human folly. We underestimate the impact of social situations upon others' behavior—we are too quick to assume that people's actions mirror their inner dispositions and attitudes. We tend to believe repeated assertions, even if we know they are dubious.[11] We overestimate the brilliance and competence of people who by happenstance are in positions of social power, even if we know they were assigned to that position arbitrarily.[12] We often adjust what we say to please our listeners and, having done so, come to believe our altered message.[13] If someone in a group is made salient—either by having us look at the person or by appearing different from the rest of the group—we tend to see that someone as causing whatever happens.[14]

We could extend the list of thinking errors, but I trust this has been a sufficient glimpse at the ease with which and the manner in which people come to believe what isn't true. The threat to our vanity posed by research on the limits and fallacies of human thought is amplified by the fact that most of the participants in these experiments were highly intelligent people, generally students at leading universities. The investigators might have gathered uneducated people and then set about to show them fools. To their credit, they instead studied people who, one might assume, ought to be immune to illusory thinking, if anyone is. Yet these predictable distortions and biases occurred even when the people were motivated by monetary incentives to think optimally. The illusions "have a persistent quality not unlike that of perceptual illusions," concludes Paul Slovic.[15]

Have these experiments just been playing intellectual tricks on the hapless participants, thus making their intuitions look worse than they are? In their important new book, *Human Inference: Strategies and Shortcomings in Human*

Judgment, Richard Nisbett and Lee Ross contend that, if anything, the laboratory procedures overestimate our intuitive powers.[16] The experiments usually present people with clear evidence and forewarn them that their reasoning ability is being tested. Seldom does life say to us: "Here is some evidence. Now put on your intellectual Sunday best and answer these questions." Often our everyday failings are inconsequential, but not always so. As the remaining chapters will emphasize, false impressions, interpretations, and beliefs can produce serious consequences.

Since we know that these errors even creep into sophisticated scientific thinking, it seems safe to conclude that none of us is exempt from them. Because we usually get little objective feedback about the truth of our beliefs (and when we do get disconfirming news we have ways of discounting or reinterpreting it), most of us manage to remain oblivious to our illusory thinking. Apparently human nature had not changed since 3000 years ago when the Psalmist observed that "no one can see his own errors."[17] As Winston Churchill wryly observed, "Man will occasionally stumble over the truth, but most of the time he will pick himself up and continue on."

Lest we succumb to the cynical conclusion that *all* beliefs are absurd, I hasten to balance the picture. The elegant analyses of the imperfections of our thinking are themselves a tribute to human wisdom. Were I to argue that *all* human thought is illusory, my assertion would be self-refuting, for it, too, would be but an illusion. The idea that reality is nothing but an inkblot onto which we project our invented beliefs self-destructs, because it necessitates that this idea is itself nothing more than another fabrication.

Just as medical science has found it a useful working assumption that any given body organ exists to serve a function, so have behavioral scientists found it useful to assume that our modes of thought and behavior are generally adaptive. The rules of thought which produce so many false convictions and such striking deficiencies in our statistical intuition often serve us well. Frequently, the errors are a by-product of our mind's strategies for simplifying the complex information it receives. This parallels our perceptual mechanisms, which usually give us a useful image of the world, but which will sometimes produce visual illusions.

Our vulnerability to illusory beliefs sometimes facilitates our survival. The belief in one's power to control events helps maintain hope and effort where despair might otherwise prevail. If things are sometimes subject to control and sometimes not, we will maximize our outcomes by "possibility thinking." There is wisdom in presuming that outcomes are produced by the acts which precede them, because this is often true; believing in the power of our acts encourages us to maximize our influence upon the environment. Optimistic thinking pays dividends and therefore has probably been selected and retained during the history of our species.

Research in cognitive social psychology mirrors the mixed review given humanity in the Bible.[18] Many research psychologists have spent lifetimes exploring the awesome capacities of the human mind. We image-bearers of the infinite and omniscient mind are capable of great achievements and impressive insights into nature. We're smart enough to have sent someone to the moon (although far from being the product of one human's brilliant intuition, the moon landing was a massive application of scientific methodology). But our brilliance in some situations seems matched by our foolishness in others. Our intention is more vulnerable to error than, intuitively, we suspect. With rather incredible ease, we form and sustain false beliefs.

CHAPTER 7

ESP and the Paranormal Phenomena Phenomenon

If the distortions and fabrications of the human mind are as pervasive as I have maintained, then they will have penetrated all realms of human thought. For illustrative purposes, I have chosen two domains where, in our day, illusory thinking seems especially evident: belief in ESP, and belief in the validity of psychological descriptions and explanations of people's personalities.[1]

Pied Pipers need only pipe today and the gullible public will follow. Our culture is fascinated with claims that defy scientific explanation. Devotees of Edgar Cayce and Jeane Dixon, and believers in dream telepathy, out-of-body experiences, psychokinesis, astrology, demonology, levitation, reincarnation, horoscopes, and ghosts all know that prejudice sometimes prevents scientists from recognizing unexpected truths. Just occasionally a mind-boggling claim turns out to be true.

When confronted with extraordinary claims, we are therefore vulnerable to two errors. Being totally skeptical of all extraordinary claims will sometimes lead us to reject truth. During the eighteenth century, scientists scoffed at the notion that meteorites had extraterrestrial origins. When two Yale scientists dared deviate from the conventional opinion, Thomas Jefferson responded, "Gentlemen, I would rather believe that those two Yankee Professors would lie than to believe that stones fell from heaven."[2] Twenty years ago how many of us would have believed claims for cosmic black holes and ethereal subatomic particles? On the other hand, naiveté can make us gullible to all sorts of falsehoods. An open but critical stance thus seems the best posture from which to sift truth from fantasy.

My primary purpose here is to show how the seductive power of illusory thinking leads to belief in paranormal phenomena, whether or not such phenomena exist. By exploiting the ways people form and perpetuate false beliefs, there is almost no limit to the fictions that can be perpetrated upon credulous minds. As P. T. Barnum reportedly concluded, "no one has ever lost money by underestimating the intelligence of the American people." But first let's review briefly some of the reasons for being skeptical about reputed paranormal phenomena. I shall take extrasensory perception (ESP), the most respectable of the paranormal claims, as a case in point.

DOUBTS ABOUT ESP

It is generally impossible to prove that any given paranormal claim is, in fact, false. Discrediting a thousand ghost stories does not disprove that, somewhere, there lurks a ghost. The most that can be said is that our scrutiny of the purported evidence for ghosts combined with all else that we know about nature inclines us to be skeptical about such claims. Likewise, it cannot be proven that no person has ever possessed ESP; the most that can be established is that many false claims have been made and that irrefutable evidence for ESP does not exist.

Parapsychologists (psychologists who study paranormal phenomena) have been plagued by a history of fraud and trickery. For years, stage performers of ESP have been converting audiences. Few performers, however, will subject themselves to competent observers, for those who do are usually debunked. The Fox sisters, well-known American mediums during the middle of the nineteenth century, could elicit strange rapping sounds by calling on an invisible spirit. In 1857, *The Boston Globe,* responding to a new wave of spiritualistic claims, offered $500 to anyone who could produce authentic spiritualistic phenomena. The Fox sisters, and all others who competed, were discredited. Yet the publicity increased their business. (Thirty years later the sisters confessed to producing the sounds by snapping their big toes.) The lesson to be learned from this, suggests Ernest Hilgard, "is the helplessness of science against committed belief, a helplessness that is shown even today after the exposure of one fraud after another."[3]

One need not be as clever as the Fox sisters. Many magic books for young children contain enough simple ESP tricks to enable any amateur to convince most adults.[4] Victor Benassi, Barry Singer, and Craig Reynolds had someone demonstrate simple tricks to introductory psychology students at a California university. Even when the students were forewarned that this was a magician who would only "pretend to read minds and demonstrate psychic abilities . . . what you'll be seeing are only tricks," a majority were convinced the performer was psychic. As some students later explained, they had now seen paranormal phenomena "with their own eyes."[5]

The most effective discrediting of such performers has come not from scientists, but from magicians who know they can fool scientists and who are irritated at those who make enormous sums of money by dishonestly exploiting their art.[6] In this century, the closest counterpart to the Fox sisters is probably Uri Geller, whose feats of spoon bending and clairvoyance have been marketed on stage and displayed before scientists. Magician James Randi, for example, has duplicated Geller's feats and offered $10,000 to anyone who can demonstrate psychic powers before a group of experts like himself. In the past fifteen years more than 300 people have tried. All have failed.

When people stake their case for ESP upon a star performer, only to find themselves taken in by fraud, they then hunger for more reputable evidence. "One is hard put to think of many parapsychologists who have *not* been Geller-gawkers," writes Martin Gardner. "I must add that in recent months their silence about Uri has become deafening as it becomes obvious that Uri has no more psi ability than [other] performers. . . ."[7] Parapsychologists have been burned by trickery often enough that most are now attempting to put ESP on a more solid foundation by demonstrating it in controlled laboratory experiments.

A recent report by Bruce Layton and Bill Turnbull illustrates the typical ESP procedure and some of the reasons why most research psycholgists are not convinced ESP exists.[8] They had a computer generate a randomized 100-item list of the digits 1, 2, 3, 4, and 5 for each of 179 students in their experiment. All participants were given a sealed envelope containing their list and were asked to guess which number was in each of the 100 positions. The expected number of "hits" was 20 out of 100. Although most of the statistical tests yielded results attributable merely to chance, some did not. For example, when the experimenter introduced the task by suggesting that ESP has beneficial effects, 20.66 hits were obtained on the average; when it was suggested that ESP is harmful, only 19.49 hits were obtained. Since a difference this large would be expected by chance only 6 times in 100, Layton and Turnbull submitted their evidence for ESP to the hard-nosed *Journal of Experimental Social Psychology.* Judging the research to have been competently conducted, yet also troubled by the controversial and ambiguous results, the editor responded by making an unusual offer which Layton and Turnbull accepted. Layton and Turnbull would repeat their experiment and report the findings, regardless of outcome; the journal would publish the results of both experiments, regardless of the outcome of the replication. The result of the second experiment, in Layton and Turnbull's own words, "can be summarized rather succinctly: no significant effects were present." Another research psychologist, Anthony Greenwald, combined the results from both the Layton and Turnbull experiments, encompassing 414 people, and found that the data almost perfectly fitted the distribution one would expect if ESP does not exist. [9]

The Layton-Turnbull case illustrates five facts about ESP research and its standing within the scientific community. First, researchers who believe in ESP and who want to demonstrate it are, for the most part, seekers of truth whose integrity can be trusted. Although the results of the second experiment were an embarrassment to Layton and Turnbull, they were willing to let the truth of their experiment be known.

Second, the many more researchers who are skeptical of ESP are, for the most part, open to investigations of it and are also quite willing to let the facts speak for themselves. Their irritation surfaces mostly when grandiose claims are made and the public is taken in by charlatans and exploitative media. Scientists are not fond of those who peddle "pseudoscience."

Third, the claims for ESP by responsible parapsychologists are modest—Layton and Turnbull claimed an ESP effect of less than 2% above the chance rate of 20% in their "best" subcondition. It would be foolish for any ESP proponent to claim much more than this small effect. Since the Las Vegas casinos return 95% of the money they take in, any "gifted" psychic who could beat chance by even 10% could make a living off the gambling industry. The casino owners, who perform ESP experiments every night of the week, have ceased to worry about the possibility that there are people out there who have a psychic ability to predict or influence the roll of the dice. All the mental effort exerted by gamblers does not enable them to beat chance.

Fourth, ESP is, at best, elusive. "Sensitive" ESP subjects usually "lose" their ESP gift. "This drop in scores, called the decline effect, is perhaps the most reliable and consistent aspect of parapsychology," reports John Beloff, past president of the international Parapsychological Association.[10] Moreover, unlike most other psychological phenomena in which we put stock, ESP is unreliable. If it exists it appears sporadically, usually only when skeptical scientists and magicians are not there to see it. After all the experiments on parapsychology we still do not know how to produce ESP effects. Even parapsychologist Beloff acknowledges that "no experiment showing the clear existence of the paranormal has been consistently repeated by other investigators in other laboratories with the same results." In other areas of science, such unreliability will discredit a theory (since replicability is one of the first canons of science). Persi Diaconis, a professional magician and Stanford University statistician, has closely scrutinized some well-known ESP experiments and found them "poorly designed, badly run, and inappropriately analyzed."[11] When tightly controlled, as was the Layton and Turnbull study, ESP effects, if found, are minimal and unreliable.

In response to the charge of unreliability, parapsychologists point out that their studies show significant ESP effects far more often than one would expect by chance alone. Greenwald explains this by pointing out that parapsychologists tend to publish only significant results. The published research on ESP is but a small fraction of the total research. If parapsychologists, like other psychologists, are several times more likely to submit for publication a report of research that has significant results than one with less newsworthy results, then we cannot tell from the published literature what the total pattern of results has been. The problem is further amplified by the tendency of journal editors to prefer articles with statistically significant results to those without. Would Layton and Turnbull have been as likely to submit their first experiment, and would the journal editors have been as willing to accept it, if no intriguing results had been obtained? This problem with our publication system is, to be sure, not unique to ESP research, but it does plague the parapsychology literature.[12]

Finally, the negative results which Layton and Turnbull obtained in their second experiment (and in their two experiments combined) apparently did not weaken their belief in ESP. Surely, they reasoned, there must have been some subtle differences between their two experiments. "Given a better defined theory of psi, it would have been possible to know in advance which variables were critical and which not," they surmised. This statement illustrates the resilience of beliefs, even of scientific beliefs, to disconfirming information. This problem, like the publication problem, is not unique to parapsychologists, but neither are they exempt from this human tendency.

When one adds to the foregoing considerations the fact that what we know about the dependence of mind upon the physical brain is evidence against the notion that the mind could operate apart from the brain, belief in ESP, in truly extrasensory communication, seems fanciful; it borders on the irrational. Perhaps, however, I have not proven to your satisfaction that ESP does not exist. Such would not surprise me; I have not proven it to myself either. So, let me try a less ambitious assertion: *Even if there is no ESP, the mental illusions described earlier almost guarantee that humanity would invent such a belief.* People's tendencies to oversimplify reality—to make false proclamations about what they have done and why they did it; to have difficulty assessing the workings of their minds; to be overconfident about their intuitions; to notice, interpret, and recall events which confirm their expectations; to be overly persuaded by unrepresentative anecdotes; and to miss the distinction between coincidence and causation—form nature's recipe for convincing gullible minds of phenomena that may not exist. To illustrate, let us recall some of these illusory thought processes.

WHY PEOPLE BELIEVE IN ESP

People's beliefs in ESP illustrate the mind's tendency to be easily persuaded by vivid experiences and amazing anecdotes that seem to defy coincidence and to have no other obvious explanation. An extraordinary personal experience may instantly override skepticism. The person then clings to this felt truth, even if, when a community of inquirers tries to probe the phenomenon, it evaporates. Thus belief in the paranormal is now normal: 58% of Americans in one recent national survey said they had "personally experienced" ESP.

There are several reasons why people may draw erroneous conclusions from their experiences. First, people often fail to consciously detect what has influenced them. This leaves them free to concoct false explanations for their experiences. Second, the deficiencies in people's mathematical hunches lead them to see unusual events as almost impossible. When asked the chances of at least two persons in a group of 30 having the same birthday, people usually will grossly underestimate the correct answer—7 in 10. Our failure to recognize chance occurrences for what they are predisposes us to seek extraordinary explanations for ordinary events.

The mass media, which thrive more by entertaining than by informing, exploit our susceptibility to these illusions. The *National Enquirer* invited readers to submit their predictions of events during 1977. The 1500 resulting entries in their ESP contest were sealed in a bank vault until January 1978, whereupon they were examined and the "amazing winner" was identified. In "a stunning display of psychic ability," Mrs. Florentine Von Rad-Keyye Kaiser scored "5 out of 5 psychic predictions."[13] Setting aside the temptation to misremember vague predictions in light of what one knows has actually happened (a type of hindsight bias), we need only consider the objective probability that among 1500 entrants there would be at least a small number who would have chanced onto some accurate predictions. If 1500 people are set to flipping coins, nearly 50 will come up with five heads in a row. If you set a computer to randomly generating 1500 matchups and final scores for the next Super Bowl game, the best few among these could be selected to provide a "stunning display of the computer's psychic ability." The point of this example is not just to show how easily one can demolish spectacular claims (every belief system has its exploiters), but to illustrate how deficiencies in our statistical intuition can deceive us all.

The illusions of causation, correlation, and personal control compound the problem by leading people to perceive phenomena that really aren't there. Fred Ayeroff and Robert Abelson used these illusions to manufacture a false belief in ESP among their Yale students.[14] On each of 100 occasions, one student tried to transmit mentally one of five possible symbols to another student who guessed at what was transmitted. Both the sender and receiver then indicated whether they were confident or not confident that a "hit" had been scored. In all conditions of the experiment, the ESP success rate was nearly identical to the chance rate of 20%. Nevertheless, when students were drawn into the drama of the experiment by choosing their symbols and being given a "warm-up" period before the experiment began, they were "confident" that ESP was transpiring more than 50% of the time.

The illusion of control is conducive to other superstitions as well. Superstition, a rather crude science by which people try to manipulate natural forces to their benefit, is especially evident among people of lower socioeconomic levels whose ability to control their environment by other means is limited, and in times of economic and social stress when people grasp at anything that might ward off tragedy.[15] One recent study found that the number of German magazine articles on astrology and the occult was associated with fluctuations in the German unemployment level across the years 1918 to 1940—when unemployment was high, interest in astrology increased.[16]

The fact that people notice, perceive, interpret, and recall events in ways which sustain their existing ideas has clear implications for beliefs in paranormal phenomena. Given humanity's lack of insight into these intellective deficiencies, it is almost inevitable that people will trust their intuition more than they ought. Thus if a false belief in ESP emerges, there is every reason to expect its perpetuation. If a person has a premonition of someone's death, the premonition is recalled only if the person dies, thus easily creating an intuitive conviction that premonitions correlate with events. Jeane Dixon's hitting upon a correct prediction commands our attention. But how many recall that at the beginning of 1978 she predicted that Pope Paul would live the year with vigor (he died) or that the Panama Canal treaties would not be approved (they were)?

Recall our earlier consideration of how we reconstruct our memories with the aid of our current knowledge. Memory reconstruction is one reason for distrusting the recollections of people who have had "near-death" experiences and of medical staff who, when interviewed, reconstruct a memory of the reconstructed memories of their near-death patients. (In *The Human Puzzle* I suggest other reasons for doubting the significance of near-death experiences.) Unaware of memory reconstruction, people are easily fooled. Ernest Hilgard, no doubter of hypnotic phenomena, describes how reports of extreme age regressions under hypnosis unwittingly incorporate shreds of people's forgotten past experience. The case of Bridey Murphy received tremendous publicity during the 1950s and was the subject of a best-selling book. Under hypnosis, Virginia Tighe, a housewife, assumed the personality and Irish brogue of a girl, Bridey Murphy, who claimed to be her previous incarnation. After considerable controversy over the reincarnation evidence, two enterprising reporters in Chicago looked into Virginia's background.

> With the help of Rev. Wally White, pastor of the Chicago Gospel Tabernacle where Virginia attended Sunday School, it did not take them long to locate Mrs. Anthony Corkell. Now a widow with seven children, she was living in the old frame house where she had lived when Virginia was in her teens. For five years Virginia lived in a basement apartment across the street. Mrs. Corkell's Irish background had fascinated the little girl. One of her friends recalled that Virginia even had a "mad crush" on John, one of the Corkell boys. Another Corkell boy was named Kevin, the name of one of the imaginary Bridey's friends. Note also the similarity of Corkell and Cork, the city where Bridey was supposed to have lived. And what was Mrs. Corkell's maiden name? Bridie (with an "ie") Murphy![17]

With the aid of some forgotten childhood experiences, Mrs. Tighe had managed to construct an imaginary past and to convince herself, her hypnotist, and a worldwide following of its authenticity.

Am I being unfair to the psychics by selectively recalling embarrassing examples? Is my bias opposite to the believer's selective recall of successful predictions? Here are some predictions for the future, drawn from a survey of 100 of the "world's most gifted seers" and reported in the March 13, 1979 *National Enquirer.* I am writing this on March 12, 1979. So, from this vantage point, you who read this are living in the future. Some predictions seem likely to be fulfilled. Eighty-five percent of the psychics believe Billy Carter will continue to embarrass his brother, which at this point sounds like predicting that Jimmy Carter will continue to smile. Some predictions are sufficiently ambiguous that, regardless of what happens, people could easily recall events which seem to confirm the expectation. For example, 82% forecast a strengthening of the family unit. But some predictions are both precise and sufficiently improbable to be useful. Eighty-five of the 100 gifted psychics "predict a major break-through in cancer treatment within months—and many see the advance almost totally wiping out the disease." Eighty-one "predict startling contact with alien beings this year." In addition to answering questions posed on these topics, the psychics volunteered their own predictions for 1979—that Jimmy Hoffa's body will be discovered, that Robert Redford will be involved in a serious car crash, that King Hussein of Jordan will survive an assassination attempt in New York, and that Elizabeth Taylor will survive hospitalization for pneumonia. I am content to leave it to you dwellers in the future to look back and evaluate these psychic predictions. How many were fulfilled in 1979?

In addition to various deficiencies in the processing and recollection of information, people may be *motivated* to believe in ESP. Recall that in the biblical view, humanity's basic sin is its disinclination to recognize its creaturely limitations and dependence upon God. This pride seems evident in the yearning for God-like omniscience—reading other people's minds and foretelling the future. We are constantly tempted to forget the reminder in Isaiah that "I am God; there is none like me." "The divine is within us," occult philosophy teaches. A film on "The Amazing World of Psychic Phenomena" recently broadcast on NBC concluded by encouraging this bent toward self-deification:

> If we learn to channel our latent powers we may be able to alter the future in a way that we now can only imagine. We might, perhaps, think of communicating across the great barren stretches of outer space using telepathy . . . We are energy, made of the same stuff as the stars. We are energy and we are forever.

By contrast, the Jewish and Christian heritage assumes that human beings are, in Seward Hiltner's words, creatures of God, beings other than he, and not, as some religions have declared, pieces of or emanations of God . . . The Jews saw a kind of connection between finitude and sin. The original sin appeared when human creatureliness and finitude were denied rather than accepted. . . . Rebellion may still take the form of denying our creaturehood, trying to make God unnecessary, or trying to live, as Reinhold Niebuhr put it, as if one had conquered all his limitations.[18]

Although many Christian writers have touted ESP as scientific proof of a God-like nonmaterial essence in human nature, books along these lines are usually a product of ignorance— ignorance about the scientific status of ESP and ignorance of the biblical view that human nature is a bounded mind-body unity. Science, by debunking the self-deifying claims of seers and psychics, sides with biblical religion. The Bible reminds us constantly that our final hope must be not in ourselves (by presuming that we possess omniscient mental powers and an inherently immortal nature), but in a being who created and accepts our limits and who promises to re-create us in a new life that will have no end.

Many observers of occult belief have speculated one other motivation for it: a yearning for mystery in an age when religious faith has waned and science seems to be demystifying our existence. Archbishop William Temple commented that when people cease to believe in God, they do not believe in nothing, they believe in anything. "That 'nature abhors a vacuum' is true in the spiritual realm as well as in the physical realm," suggests Charles Huttar. "If man is no longer permitted to have faith, he will embrace superstition."[19]

To divert our attention from humdrum life, pseudoscience replaces real mysteries with phony ones. It displaces science with science fiction. When the aura of science is combined with the mystique of religion, the ensuing illusions can easily become an opiate of the people. Rather than humbling us with genuine mysteries like the eternity of time, the infinity of space, the mind-boggling infrastructure of matter and life, the improbability of our own existence, and the mysteries of our own inner nature, the result is often deification of human nature—another reenactment of original sin.

The remedy is not only to expose the intellectual bankruptcy of beliefs in paranormal phenomena, as I have sought to do here, but also to cultivate an awareness of the genuine mysteries and their implications for our view of life. The creation contains mystery enough for human imagination without our having to invent pseudomysteries. Physicists tell us about strange, nonsubstantive realities and describe them with contradictory, but seemingly valid, theories. Psychologists are only beginning to fathom the awesome process by which the human brain assembles neural impulses into a visual perception. Our minds cannot comprehend how the universe was begun out of nothing, or alternatively, how it could exist without beginning. We cannot grasp a cosmic space that has no end, nor one that does. Brilliant theologians are still struggling to understand how God could be both the sovereign creator-sustainer of all that exists and judge of his own creation. Reflecting upon awesome and baffling puzzles such as these is mystery enough. Far from feeding our pride, these grand mysteries of modern science and theology remind us of our finiteness and our ultimate dependence upon the author of them all.

Now and then our suppressed sense that we are merely creatures, limited in wisdom and living under sentence of death, breaks through to consciousness, and we grope to find meaning behind the apparent absurdity of it all. The *Humanist* magazine has been strenuously countering superstitious beliefs, and yet these very beliefs are partly a response to the failure of naturalistic humanism to satisfy the transcendent longings of the human soul. As Paul Kurtz, editor of *Humanist*, acknowledged,

> There is a search that is fundamental to our being: the quest for meaning. The human mind has a genuine desire to plumb the depths

CHAPTER 8

Fallacious Personality Interpretation

It is easy to identify the illusory beliefs of eras and groups *other* than our own. We delight in seeing the pretensions of others punctured, but we draw back with considerable defensiveness when the pin pricks our own. Many of us are already inclined to be skeptical about paranormal phenomena, but we are considerably more trusting of our ability to judge people's personalities. Some people surely *are* quite sensitive and perceptive. However, if illusory thinking taints *all* domains of human thought, then we are probably also susceptible to it as we characterize others and receive psychological analyses of ourselves.

AMATEUR PSYCHOLOGIZING

Because we lack insight into our own thinking, we are sometimes unaware of what influences our judgments of others. Richard Nisbett and Nancy Bellows had people first read what was described as a woman's job application folder.[1] While perusing the folder, they were either informed or not informed that the woman (1) was physically attractive, (2) had an excellent academic record, (3) had spilled coffee during her interview, (4) had been in a car accident, and/or (5) would later be introduced to them. Next, the people judged the woman's characteristics and assessed which of the five factors had influenced their judgments. As Nisbett and Bellows expected, the people accurately recognized that their judgments of her intelligence were strongly influenced by her academic record, an obviously relevant factor. However, when the factor was less obviously related to the trait being judged, the people inaccurately assessed what had influenced their judgments. Virtually no relationship existed between how much the five factors had influenced their judgments of her likability, empathy, and flexibility and how much they *thought* the factors had influenced them, demonstrating that at least some of the time we are grossly insensitive to how the qualities and actions of other people have molded our impressions of them.

There are several additional reasons why our everyday assessments of people are prone to error. When explaining others' behavior, we typically underappreciate the impact of situational forces and overestimate the impact of the person's attitudes and inner personality.[2] Social psychologists call this the "fundamental attribution error." In a laboratory demonstration of the principle, Lee Ross and his colleagues randomly assigned some students to play the role of questioner and some to play the role of contestant in a simulated quiz game.[3] The questioners were to demonstrate their knowledge by making up difficult, esoteric questions. Everyone was aware that the questioner had the advantage. Yet, both participants and observers succumbed to the erroneous impression that the questioners *really were* more knowledgeable than the contestants; they attributed the contestants' inability to answer the questions to the contestants' lack of knowledge rather than to their being assigned a role in which they were not as able to demonstrate their knowledge as was the questioner. In everyday life, people in positions of social power, such as teachers and business executives, ask many questions of their underlings. This may lead the underlings to commit the "fundamental attribution error," by overestimating the brilliance of their superiors.

We all have what researchers call "implicit personality theories" or "schemas"—"salespeople are extroverted," "show people are egocentric," "scholars are reclusive." Once formed, these theories and stereotypes are easily perpetuated in ways usually unnoticed. People will "pick up only what they have schemas for," writes Ulric Neisser, "and willy-nilly ignore the rest."[4] We stereotype partly as a simple result of our tendency to categorize. Thus stereotyping is a by-product of our desire to make order out of the world. Classifying things simplifies the world. But sometimes this gives us an overly simplistic picture of a complex reality. For example, studies indicate that people tend to overestimate the similarities of items *within* categories (e.g., blacks, football players, Christians, sorority women, old people) and also to overestimate the differences *between* the categories.

Illusory thinking also contaminates our judgments of ourselves. Consider the "Barnum effect" (named in honor of P. T. Barnum who said that "There's a sucker born every minute" and that a good circus had a "little something for everybody"?). Read the following, which is intended to be a description that fits most people. How well does it fit you?

You have a very practical bent and enjoy earning money, but sometimes your deep desire to be a creative person triumphs over your practicality. You lead other people with your innovative ideas, or could do this if you felt more sure of yourself. Insecurity is your greatest weakness, and you would be wise to try to overcome this. Your deep sense of humor and warm, understanding nature win you true friends, and although they may not be numerous, you share a rather intense loyalty to each other. With your innovative mind, you rebel against authority, either inwardly or openly. Even though you could make a stable businessman, you would be a very idealistic one, finding it hard not to defend the underdog or try to settle arguments that arise. You like to think of yourself as unprejudiced, but periodically examine yourself to make sure you aren't overlooking some harmful judgments. You will live a long, full life if you take care of yourself. You love to have freedom in whatever you're doing, and this makes you dislike monotonous tasks and being in large crowds where you can't seem to move freely. If someone pays you a well-deserved compliment, you enjoy hearing it, but you may not show that you do. Sometimes you find that the actions you take do

not accomplish as much as you'd like them to, especially in dealing
with people. You have a real grasp of how people are feeling or what
they are thinking without their necessarily telling you.[5]

In many experiments, C. R. Snyder and others have shown
people such descriptions (this one constructed from a horoscope book). Told, as were you, that the information is true of
most individuals, the people usually indicate that it fits so-so.
But if told that the description is designed specifically for
them on the basis of their psychological tests or astrological
data, the people usually say the description is very accurate.
In fact, given a choice between a false generalized personality
description and a real one based on bona fide tests, people are
as likely as not to say that the phony description is the more
accurate.

People also are more inclined to accept false results
supposedly derived from projective tests (like the Rorschach
inkblots) than from a less subjective procedure, and having
accepted the phony results, they express increased confidence in psychological testing and in the skill of their
clinician. Richard Petty and Timothy Brock have found that
people also live up to assessments provided by a psychologist.
People told that "You are an open-minded person. You have
the ability to see both sides of an issue" later wrote a fairly
balanced assessment of two issues. Those told that "You are
not a wishy-washy person. . . . You can take a strong stand on
one side and defend it" wrote one-sided assessments of the
issues.[6]

People see these "Barnum descriptions" as more true of
themselves than of people in general, especially when the
description is positive. In their eagerness to accept positive
feedback, people tend to throw caution to the wind; they
readily believe the description regardless of whether it is said
to come from an experienced clinician, their fellow students,
a psychological test, or a horoscope. Do people ever distinguish between credible and nontrustworthy sources? Yes—

when the feedback is negative![7] Here, then, is yet more evidence of the enormity of human pride. Within reason, the more favorable a phony description is, the more we believe it and the more likely we are to perceive it as unique to ourselves.[8]

In summary, we lay people are often . . .

· unaware of what has influenced our assessments of others,
· vulnerable to the "fundamental attribution error,"
· prone to perceiving people in line with our stereotypes, and
· susceptible to the "Barnum effect" (accepting worthless diagnoses).

PROFESSIONAL PSYCHOLOGIZING

People's believing horoscope data about themselves in the same way as personality test data, and their being most receptive to personality test feedback on tests that have the lowest actual validity, raises some disconcerting implications for psychiatry and clinical psychology. Regardless of whether a particular diagnosis has any validity, the recipient is likely to stand in awe of it, especially after expending effort and money to receive it. The Barnum effect suggests a recipe for impressing clients. The clinician should give people a subjective test; should make them think that its interpretation is unique to them; and, drawing upon things true of most people, tell them something that, while positive, is somewhat ambiguous. In such ways clinicians can increase a client's faith in their clinical skills—even if what the client has been told has no diagnostic validity.

A client's praise therefore does not validate a clinician's skill. Nor does praise from an audience necessarily validate a speaker's message. D. H. Naftulin, J. E. Ware, and F. A. Donnelly had "Dr. Fox," a skilled actor, give an extemporaneous lecture to a professional audience on a subject about which he was completely ignorant.[9] Though the lecture was devoid of substance and intentionally full of double-talk and contradictions, the actor's charisma elicited favorable ratings from his listeners, none of whom detected the farce.

The Barnum effect demonstrates an "illusion of uniqueness," at least for positive traits. People are more alike than they realize. Edmund Bourne has shown how our similarities can inflate the seeming accuracy of our descriptions of people.[10] When members of small, intimate groups described each other using various techniques of assessment, Bourne found that their descriptions of any given individual agreed fairly well. But after further analysis he noted that their agreement resulted mostly from impressions that they applied in general. For example, although two fraternity brothers might agree that John is more extroverted than introverted, they might also report this about fraternity men in general. When these stereotypes about people in general were extracted, Bourne found that the agreement about others' personalities fell nearly to the level of chance. Thus clinical diagnosticians, agreeing in their assessment of a particular patient is informative only to the extent that their agreement cannot be attributed to what clinicians might say about *any* patient. As Paul Meehl has noted, "It is not very illuminating to say of a known psychiatric patient that he has difficulty in accepting his drives, experiences some trouble in relating emotionally to others, and may have problems with sexuality."[11]

Mental health professionals are vulnerable to other illusions as well. Illusory correlations have perpetuated many a clinical superstition. Pioneering experiments by Loren and Jean Chapman, and many others since, have demonstrated that, after viewing a set of patients' test performances and diagnoses, both college students and professional clinicians will perceive expected associations (e.g., between particular responses to Rorschach inkblots and homosexuality) even when the expected associations are demonstrably absent or even contrary to what is expected.[12] For instance, clinicians who believe that suspicious people draw peculiar eyes on the Draw-a-Person test are likely to perceive such a relationship —even when shown cases in which suspicious people draw peculiar eyes *less* often than nonsuspicious people. This illusory correlation results from biases in our processing of information. If you were shown a series of slides in which the word pairs lion-tiger, lion-eggs, bacon-eggs, and bacon-tiger were shown equally often, you would probably overestimate the co-occurrence of the familiar lion-tiger and bacon-eggs.

Consider the following court transcript in which a psychologist (Psy) is being questioned by an attorney (Att):

Att: You asked the defendant to draw a human figure?

Psy: Yes.

Att: And this is the figure he drew for you? What does it indicate to you about his personality?

Psy: You will note this is a rear view of a male. This is very rare, statistically. It indicates hiding guilt feelings, or turning away from reality.

Att: And this drawing, a female figure, does it indicate anything to you; and, if so, what?

Psy: It indicates hostility towards women on the part of the subject. The pose, the hands on the hips, the hard-looking face, the stern expression.

Att: Anything else?

Psy: The size of the ears indicates a paranoid outlook, or hallucinations. Also, the absence of feet indicates feelings of insecurity.[13]

The illusory correlation phenomenon explains why many clinicians, such as this one, continue to believe in their test interpretations even though research casts grave doubt on them. When the clinician knows the person who has taken the test, it is easy to find things about the person in the test, thus "confirming" the usefulness of the test. Moreover, the confirmation is often reinforced by the clinician's colleagues, who themselves are often subject to the same illusions. Yet, in one study, for example, twenty experts in the analysis of human figure drawings could not discriminate drawings made by schizophrenics, neurotics, homosexuals, and "normal" college students. [14]

Illusory correlation probably also contaminates other aspects of clinical intuition. Tversky and Kahneman suggest how. A clinician hears a patient complain that he or she is tired of life. Worried about whether the patient is likely to attempt suicide, the clinician recalls not only the previous history of this patient, but also previous cases brought to mind by the present case. Several biases may affect this memory search. For example,

> Since attempted suicide is a dramatic and salient event, suicidal patients are likely to be more memorable and easier to recall than depressive patients who did not attempt suicide. As a consequence, the clinician may recall suicidal patients he has encountered and judge the likelihood of an attempted suicide by the degree of resemblance between these cases and the present patient. [15]

If the clinician recalls that past suicidal patients were nearly all similarly depressed, then a serious illusory correlation has occurred, for this actually says little about the probability of a depressed person attempting suicide. Likewise, if nearly all heroin users started out on marijuana, how much does this tell you about what marijuana smoking can lead to? (If all heroin users started out on milk, does this indicate that milk drinking can have pernicious consequences?)

In fairness to clinicians, I hasten to add that illusory correlation could also be shown at work among political analysts, historians, sportscasters, personnel directors, stock-brokers, and many other professionals, including the research psychologists who point it out. As a researcher I have often been blind to the shortcomings of my theoretical analyses. I am so eager to presume that my idea of truth is the truth that no matter how hard I try, I cannot see my own error. This has been especially evident from the editorial review process that precedes any research publication. During the last ten years I have read several dozen reviews of my own submitted research papers and have been a reviewer for several dozen others. My experience is that it is far easier to spot someone else's sloppy thinking than to perceive my own equally sloppy thinking.

In our psychological society a speculative psychology-of-the-gaps pops up everywhere to "explain" human behaviors not yet explainable scientifically. If we do not understand something we often invent an explanation. Oedipal interpretations of homosexuality, existential theories of the popularity of *Star Wars*, and psychodynamic explanations of Richard Nixon's enigmatic behavior are offered to a public that can hardly be expected to discriminate psychology's hunches from its established facts. After-the-fact psychologizing is especially vulnerable to the hindsight bias. Therefore, the Freudian psychological autopsies which "psychohistorians" perform on famous personalities from Martin Luther to Richard Nixon are offered with little fear of being proven wrong. Knowing how the person turned out, psychohistorians can easily give an after-the-fact interpretation of childhood experience that confirms their theory.

David Rosenhan and seven colleagues demonstrated the extent of such hindsight bias when, after giving false names and vocations, they gained admission to mental hospitals by complaining they were hearing voices.[16] During the clinical interviews they otherwise reported honestly their life histories and emotional states. Most got diagnosed as schizophrenic. Thus the clinicians searched for and easily found incidents in their (normal) life histories and hospital behavior that "confirmed" and "explained" the diagnosis. For example, Rosenhan tells of one pseudo-patient who truthfully explained to the interviewer that he

> had a close relationship with his mother but was rather remote from his father during his early childhood. During adolescence and beyond, however, his father became a close friend, while his relationship with his mother cooled. His present relationship with his wife was characteristically close and warm. Apart from occasional angry exchanges, friction was minimal. The children had rarely been spanked.

The interviewer, "knowing" the person was "schizophrenic," "explained" the problem this way:

> This white 39-year-old male . . . manifests a long history of considerable ambivalence in close relationships, which begins in early childhood. A warm relationship with his mother cools during his adolescence. A distant relationship with his father is described as becoming very intense. Affective stability is absent. His attempts to control emotionality with his wife and children are punctuated by angry outbursts and, in the case of the children, spankings. And while he says that he has several good friends, one senses considerable ambivalence embedded in those relationships also.

Rosenhan later told some mental hospital staff members (who had heard about his experiment but doubted such mistakes could occur in their hospital) that during the ensuing three months one or more pseudopatients would seek admission to their hospital. After the three months, he asked the staff to guess which of the 193 patients admitted during that time were really pseudopatients. Although there were actually none, 41 of the 193 new patients were accused by at least one staff member of being normal.

Other clinical interpretations also show the hindsight bias. When a child we know has a problem, it is easy to spot its source in parental mishandling—even if this means ignoring that parents of normal children often handle their children similarly. An interpretation that "jealousy over the new baby has created deep insecurity" is hard to disprove and easy to find confirming evidence for—once we look for it. Robert Coles's biting criticism of psychological interpretation seems appropriate:

> The psychological banalities of this century have become for some people truths, if not articles of virtual worship. Even worse, those banalities tend to be exclusionary—cruel weapons, wielded in the name—of all ironies—of charity and love, the all-too-precise, if not arrogant, psychological categorizations that are used by so many of us to dismiss, refute, or chastise others, or to show how smart and clever and well-educated we are—a contemporary version, alas, of the sin of pride.[17]

Recent research makes it increasingly apparent that children's individual traits are actually less environmentally plastic and more genetically influenced than is generally appreciated.[18] But it will be a long while before this research displaces our cultural ideology that childhood experience determines adult personality. It is noteworthy that other cultures, observing the same human reality, have developed and perpetuated different beliefs about the origins of personality.[19] Children may be seen as a product of their communities or of the genes they inherited from their parents. Cultural theories of personality are resilient to disconfirmation partly because, as we earlier noted, the very act of explaining and defending a belief enables one to understand how it *might* be true, and thus to continue to believe it even if the data which inspired it are discredited.

How this phenomenon might exaggerate clinicians' self-confidence was shown by Lee Ross and his collaborators.[20] Ross had people read actual clinical case histories, and then told some of them that a particular event later occurred (e.g., suicide) and asked them to use the case history to explain this event. Finally, they were informed that there actually was no available information about the patient's later life. When the people were then asked to estimate the likelihood of the occurrence of several possible events, including the one they had explained, the event they had explained now seemed quite likely. In another study some of their Stanford University students were led to think they had excellent clinical intuition (based on their ability to distinguish authentic suicide notes from fictitious ones). After they explained their success, they were informed that the positive feedback was false. However, since this still left the students with the reasons they had conjured up to explain their apparent success (their empathy, their insights gained from reading a novelist who committed suicide, etc.), the students maintained their inflated belief in their clinical intuition. Clearly, then, the mere activity of explaining and interpreting (in which clinicians are engaged constantly) may itself contribute to overconfidence in one's judgments.

People can also be induced to give information that fulfills their clinicians' expectations. In a clever series of experiments, Mark Snyder and William Swann gave interviewers hypotheses to test concerning possible personal traits of other individuals.[21] Typically the interviewers treated the target individuals as if they had the hypothesized trait. For example, the questions interviewers planned to use in testing for extraversion could hardly have been better calculated to elicit extraverted answers (e.g., "What would you do if you wanted to liven things up at a party?"), and likewise if the person was to be tested for introversion (e.g., "What factors make it hard for you to really open up to people?"). Targets being tested for extraversion therefore actually behaved more sociably, while people tested for introversion acted more shy and reserved. Snyder concluded that even if someone doubted an erroneous diagnosis enough to go and test it, "one would nevertheless be particularly likely to find all the evidence that one needs to confirm and retain these beliefs."[22] Seek and ye shall find.

All this new research on clinical judgment fits well with the conclusions Lewis R. Goldberg reached in 1968.[23] Research on clinical judgment has consistently confirmed, Goldberg concluded, that judgmental accuracy is not affected by amount of professional training or experience, by the amount of information available to the clinician, or by the clinician's self-confidence. To give just one example, Stuart Oskamp found that clinicians' confidence in their judgments increased as more information was made available, but without any corresponding increase in their actual accuracy.[24]

Most clinicians and interviewers thus express considerably more confidence in their intuitive assessments than in statistical data. Yet when intuitive prediction is matched against statistical prediction the latter usually does as well or better.[25] Computer-based predictions are unreliable, but human intuition is even more unreliable. Consider the assessment of human potential by graduate admissions interviewers. Robyn Dawes illustrates why statistical prediction is so often superior to an interviewer's intuition when predicting certain outcomes such as academic success.

> What makes us think that we can do a better job of selection by interviewing [students] for a half hour, than we can by adding together relevant (standardized) variables, such as undergraduate GPA, GRE score, and perhaps ratings of letters of recommendation. The most reasonable explanation to me lies in our overevaluation of our cognitive capacity. And it is really cognitive conceit. Consider, for example, what goes into a GPA. Because for most graduate applicants it is based on at least 3½ years of undergraduate study, it is a composite measure arising from a minimum of 28 courses and possibly, with the popularity of the quarter system, as many as 50. . . . Surely not all these evaluations are systematically biased against independence and creativity. Yet you and I, looking at a folder or interviewing someone for a half hour, are supposed to be able to form a better impression than one based on 3½ years of the cumulative evaluations of 20–40 different professors. Moreover, as pointed out by Rorer (1972), what you and I are doing implies an ability to assess applicant characteristics that will predict future behavior differently from past behavior; otherwise, why not just use past behavior as the predictor? Those who decry the "dehumaniza-

tion" of admitting people on the basis of past record are clearly implying such an ability. . . . Finally, if we do wish to ignore GPA, it appears that the only reason for doing so is believing that the candidate is particularly brilliant even though his or her record may not show it. What better evidence for such brilliance can we have than a score on a carefully devised aptitude test? Do we really think we are better equipped to assess such aptitude than is the Educational Testing Service, whatever its faults . . . ?[26]

What effect has all this research had on the practice of clinical psychology? "Almost zilch," concludes Dawes.

Clinicians continue to give Rorschachs and TATs, to interpret statistically unreliable differences on subtests of the WAIS with abandon, and to attempt clinical integration of the data. The belief that clinicians somehow can do better than a statistical model, can integrate the information from such diverse sources into a reasonable picture of their clients, persists despite lack of supporting evidence.[27]

In summary, the evidence suggests that professional clinicians . . .

- can easily convince clients of worthless diagnoses,
- are frequently the victims of illusory correlation,
- are too readily convinced of their own after-the-fact analyses,
- fail to appreciate how erroneous diagnoses can be self-confirming, and
- do not make better judgments with more training or self-confidence.

To conclude on a more upbeat note, research on illusory thinking hints at ways in which clinical judgment might be improved. Goldberg, for example, has experimented with training clinicians to improve their judgmental skills.[28] If clinical intuition is poor because clinicians seldom receive immediate feedback on the accuracy of their assessments, because, when they do get feedback, illusory correlations induce them to "learn" relationships that do not exist, and because information is not organized to allow systematic disconfirmation or verification of their assessments, then one can take steps to counteract these problems. The end result of Goldberg's advice is getting clinicians to supplement their clinical expertise with the analytical methods of good research.

CHAPTER 9

Conclusions

Research on illusory thinking has significant implications for theology, for psychology, and for each of us, personally. Here briefly, is my sense of these implications. I present these thoughts not as the last word, but rather in the hope that they will stimulate readers to form their own conclusions.

IMPLICATIONS FOR THEOLOGY

First, these experiments help us understand the biblical contention that "this world's wisdom is foolishness."[1] In doing so they speak to a continuing controversy in Protestant Christianity between Arminian and Reformed theology. Arminian theology, named after Jacobus Arminius, a sixteenth-century Dutch theologian who taught that humans have the capacity to choose their salvation freely, was influential in the development of early Methodism. Today this view is assumed by those evangelicals who emphasize the necessity for people to decide their own conversion—hence the Billy Graham magazine is entitled *Decision.*

The Reformation theology of Martin Luther and John Calvin places less emphasis upon the human act of decision and more emphasis on salvation as an act of God, given through his grace. According to Arminian theology, *I choose God*, a view expressed in the 1970s' bumper sticker "I found it." After I decide to believe, God will make me one of his children. In Reformed theology, *God chooses me* and, with the illumination of his Spirit, enables me to respond.

Theologian James Daane has observed that the Arminian emphasis on human decision is undergirded by an assumption of human rationality. This view of human will, "so sound and healthy as to be able to decide for Christ without benefit of regeneration, does not have a radically serious view of sin. . . . Man's reason is sound, healthy and intact, even after the fall."[2] By contrast, the Reformers taught that human reason is fallen, radically corrupted, and incapable of rationally weighing the evidence and deciding for God. The mounting evidence of the limits and errors of our unaided reason thus seems entirely congenial to Reformed theology but challenges one of the pillars of Arminian theology.

Evidence concerning the fallibility of human thinking also has implications for our attitude toward *all* theologies. While I may believe that Reformed theology is remarkably adequate to the facts as social psychologists see them, I must also remember that theology is a fallible human enterprise. "The great curse of every propositional theology has been the implicit or explicit identification of the theologian's propositional statements with God's words," notes Jack Rogers.[3]

Christians would do well to adopt the attitude of science, which in its ideal form involves profound humility. Theology at its best is like science at its best—ever reforming its always imperfect models. Archbishop Anthony Bloom put it this way in his book, *God and Man*:

> At the root of the scientist's activity there is the certainty that what he is doubting is the model he has invented—that is, the way in which he has projected his intellectual structures on the world around him and on the facts; the way in which his intelligence has grouped things. But what he is also absolutely certain of is that the reality which is beyond his model is in no danger if his model collapses. The reality is stable, it is there; the model is an inadequate expression of it, but the reality doesn't alter because the model shakes. . . .[4]

If we think of a scientist and a believer, then we will see that the scientist's doubt is systematic, it is surging, it is hopeful, it is joyful, it is destructive of what he has done himself because he believes in the reality that is beyond and not in the model he has constructed. As Lesslie Newbigin explained, "We must claim absoluteness and finality for Christ and his finished work, but that claim forbids us to claim absoluteness and finality for our understanding of it."[5]

If evidence concerning the ease with which we form and perpetuate false beliefs unsettles our confidence in our particular belief system, this may have the desirable effect of reminding us that Christians are called, first of all, not just to a system of words and beliefs anyway, but also to obedient life. The most important truth is found not in propositions, but in relationship, the type of relationship Jesus had in mind when instructing us that "I am the truth," and that "The truth shall set you free." This is truth which lies beyond the grasp of both empirical science and rationalistic theology. It is truth that can only be experienced, personally.

IMPLICATIONS FOR PSYCHOLOGY

The solidest piece of scientific truth I know of, the one thing about which I feel totally confident, is that we are profoundly ignorant about nature. Indeed, I regard this as the major discovery of the past 100 years of biology. . . . It is this sudden confrontation with the depth and scope of ignorance that represents the most significant contribution of 20th-century science to the human intellect. We are, at last, facing up to it. In earlier times, we either pretended to understand how things worked or ignored the problem, or simply made up stories to fill the gaps.

Lewis Thomas[6]

Psychology has crept only a little way across the edge of insight into our human condition. Ignorant of their ignorance, many psychologists are inclined to invent glib stories to fill the gaps in our understanding. If these stories are not rigorously checked against objective reality they will be

resilient to disconfirmation. More than that, intuitive observation will support them, even if they are mutually contradictory.

Research on illusory thinking therefore beckons psychologists to a new humility concerning the truth of their un-
checked speculation. It reminds research psychologists why,
in the true spirit of science, they must subject their precon-
ceptions to empirical test before propounding them as truth.
As Glenn Weaver has written, "submitting oneself to the data
of God's creation and God's action in history entails a certain
intellectual humility which forces us beyond the self-centered
tendencies of our human reason."[7] Since we can conceive
almost any theory, we must check our theories against the
facts, as best as we can discern them. By checking its
propositions about human nature with the observed facts of
human existence, as best we can discern them, theology may
be similarly strengthened. For, unlike the natural and social
sciences, theology is free to draw upon and integrate *all*
fruitful ways of knowing, whether by revelation, deductive
reason, or empirical test.

Do not misunderstand—I am *not* arguing that the scientific
method can answer all human questions. There are questions
it cannot address and ways of knowing, such as the direct
I-Thou encounter with another being, which it cannot
capture. But science *is* an appropriate means for examining
claims about nature, human nature included. Propositions
that imply observable consequences are best evaluated with
systematic observation and experiment. For today's armchair
theorists to suppose that their speculations can significantly
surpass the accumulated wisdom of past ages is simple
arrogance. To be sure, inventive genius is also required, lest
researchers test only trivialities. Moreover, ideas gained from
everyday experience feed the research process.[8] But whatever unique and enduring insights psychology can offer will be

hammered out by research psychologists sorting through competing truth claims. Science always involves an interplay between intuition and rigorous test, between creative hunches and skepticism.

Psychology will never be as exact a science as chemistry is. But psychology's distinct contribution is its objective observations and experiments, even granting that the results always require interpretation. For by now obvious reasons, psychological investigations must not rely exclusively upon people's subjective reports of the workings of their minds or of why they acted or felt as they did. We must gather information in a way analogous to how we assess our personal health. If we are having doubts about our health we will use at least two sources of information about our condition: our intuitive feelings *plus* what the lab technician's microscope may detect, even if our unaided observation could not. The experimental method is the research psychologist's microscope.

Knowing the enormity of illusory thinking therefore points not to the cynical conclusion that all beliefs are arbitrary, but to the need for a science of human thought and behavior, to the need to restrain our imagination by subjecting our speculations to empirical scrutiny. Francis Bacon, a Christian empiricist who helped shape the modern scientific method, saw the same implication of the weakness of human intuition:

> Our method and that of the sceptics agree in some respects at first setting out, but differ most widely, and are completely opposed to each other in their conclusion; for they roundly assert that nothing can be known; we, that but a small part of nature can be known, by the present method; their next step, however, is to destroy the authority of the senses and understanding, whilst we invent and supply them with assistance. [9]

We must, however, grant the skeptics this much: even after the most rigorous empirical analyses, our best established theories will never be more than tentative approximations, crude models, of the infinitely complex human reality.

PERSONAL IMPLICATIONS

Knowing our susceptibility to erroneous belief also has implications for our view of ourselves. First, it helps us better understand why Jesus cautioned us to "Judge not." Since our judgments of others are readily susceptible to error, we can easily wrong them when we spread our judgments. We can become too sure that Johnny Jones's troubles are caused by his "overprotective mother," or that our first impression of the new neighbor or the prospective employee is an accurate assessment.

Second, we ought not take ourselves too seriously, nor should we feel intimidated by people who are unwavering "true believers." The temptation to pride—to think more of ourselves and our wisdom than we ought—is ever present. If falsehoods creep into all domains of human belief, then they are bound to contaminate my ideas and yours, and the next person's, too. Not only is it therefore okay to have doubts, it is silly self-deification not to grant the likelihood of error within our belief system. Each one of us peers at reality through a glass, darkly, glimpsing only its shadowy outlines. The belief we can hold with greatest certainty is the humbling conviction that some of our beliefs contain error, which is, of course, only a way of saying that we are finite men and women, not little gods. Although we humans are always tempted to pretend God-like attributes, Christian faith proclaims these illusions unnecessary for self-esteem. It's okay to be merely human—to drop some of our pretensions and begin accepting our limits—because God accepts and loves us just as we are. That's the core idea of the gospel.

Such humility may also open us to growth in faith. As

Frederick Buechner has written, "Whether your faith is that there is a God or that there is not a God, if you don't have any doubts you are either kidding yourself or asleep. Doubts are the ants in the pants of faith. They keep it awake and moving."[10]

Is this research on pride and error *too* humbling? Do you feel an urge to exclaim with Hamlet's mother, "Speak no more: Thou turn'st mine eyes into my very soul; And there I see such black and grained spots. . . ." Are the researchers who uncover our susceptibility to error the modern counterpart to Gregers Werle in Henrik Ibsen's play *The Wild Duck*? (Werle demolished people's illusions, leaving them without hope or meaning.) A common theme of several space-age movies and television programs—*Star Wars, Battlestar Gallactica, Buck Rogers*—is that human intuition has enormous wisdom, if only we will let go of our scientific aids and trust it. Heroic events occur after the pilot of the space fighter turns off his computers and trusts his intuition. Such adulation of human intuition is wishful thinking. Surely, though, we can acknowledge the hard truth of our human limits and still sympathize with the deeper message that people are more than machines. Our subjective experiences are a large part of the stuff of our humanity—our art and our music, our enjoyment of friendship and love, our mystical and religious experiences.

The research psychologists who explore illusory thinking are not out to remake us into unfeeling, unbelieving machines. They would grant, or even insist, that intuition and feeling not only enrich human experience, but are even an important source of creative ideas. They would add, however, the humbling reminder that our susceptibility to error also makes clear the need for disciplined training of the mind. It is simply not true that intuition and feeling provide a reliable road to truth. As Norman Cousins has argued, transforming schooling into mere vocational education misses "the biggest truth of all about learning: that its purpose is to unlock the human mind and to develop it into an organ capable of thought—conceptual thought, analytical thought, sequential thought."[11]

But, alas, even this is not enough. The most educated professionals and scientists are not exempt from the illusions of human thought. Indeed, their education and the respect they are paid may make them most susceptible of all to haughty pretension. Having created an imposing, intimidating aura about themselves and having persuaded people to abdicate their own judgment to the "professional" judgment, they, of all people, may need an occasional call to humility or even, sometimes, to have their pretension punctured. In one of C. S. Lewis's *Chronicles of Narnia*, Bree, a proud talking horse, is exposed by the great lion Aslan in the midst of a confident but fallacious proclamation. "Aslan," said Bree in a shaken voice, "I'm afraid I must be rather a fool." Aslan's gentle reply: "Happy the horse who knows that while he is still young. Or the human either."[12]

PART THREE

WHERE THEN IS HOPE?

CHAPTER 10

Therapeutic Psychology

The radio commentator Gabriel Heatter began his broadcasts with "There's bad news tonight and there's good news tonight." If the bad news is that evil and illusion are more central to human existence than the modern mind appreciates, what, then, is the good news? Where is there a reassuring hope that can keep us from the pit of cynicism and despair as we confront the reality of evil and illusion? We grope in the darkness of our illusions for something to light up our lives. Yet too often we reach only for light that, like the afterimage we experience when covering our eyes, dims even as we try to sustain its vanishing beauty. "When our intellect does not conform to the reality of things," said Pope Pius XII, "it wanders in the illusion of dreams and pursues a phantom." In our age, illusory promises come most prominently from the new flood of books and programs marketing self-redemption, from exaggerated claims about the healing benefits of psychotherapy, and from the success recipes of popular religion.

DO-IT-YOURSELF PSYCHIC REPAIR

"To visit a bookstore today," observes George F. Will, "is to feel misgivings about universal literacy, which has produced a mass market for hundreds of profoundly sad handbooks on achieving happiness."[1]

One authority estimates that we now have approximately 3000 diet books, 2000 self-improvement treatises, and 1000 sex manuals available to us.[2] It's the old Pharisaic and Puritan work ethic newly applied to one's inner life. Added together these books form what commentator Lance Morrow calls "an entire I'm terrific library of aggressive narcissism." The common thread running through many of them is some prescription for feeling good about oneself. Pull a few psychic levers here and there, make-believe the best about yourself, trust your intuition, assert your impulses, and you'll become Jung at heart again. "We dig deep into everything that's fundamental to happiness and adjustment and success in living," claims an ad for *Psychology Today* magazine.

For those who prefer something more experiential, the human potential movement offers a potpourri. Those who don't go ape over primal scream groups might consider the following redemptive opportunities publicized in a recent newsletter of the Association for Humanistic Psychology:

Intensive Journal Workshops
Integration of Gestalt Therapy, Transactional Analysis, and Body Work
GRIP Psychology (Guidance Related to Individual Potential)
A Day of Massage with Hot Tub
Consciousness Evolution
Self-esteem and Romantic Relationships
Senoi Dream Education
Psychosynthesis
Total Feeling Process
Experiencing Entayant
Gestalt Bioenergetics.[3]

Factual data on the effectiveness of these manuals and programs for self-help are generally not available. Instead, their proponents offer us the persuasive power of glowing anecdotes and testimonies along with their own intuitive explanation as to *why* their plan succeeds. Never mind that this provides a made-to-order stage for the operation of illusory beliefs about causal efficacy. "I have seen how it works," one hears, and that is all the proof most people require.

Although research has not evaluated the many competing claims, several observations do seem justified. First, at the very least, many of these promises must be partly false, since these competitors for our allegiance and our money often contradict one another. Moreover, if authentic deliverance from human problems has been discovered and published, then one wonders why there still exists a continually expanding market for new solutions. When observing at a distance the popularity of Transcendental Meditation, Erhard Seminars, Silva Mind Control, and other self-help programs, a typical pattern emerges: the new salvation is announced with grand promises and much publicity; people flock to it in rapidly escalating numbers, until, eventually, interest begins to wane and people move on to the next hope. One wonders if any of these ego-Edens will be thriving twenty-five years from now, or whether history will record them all as just another vial of psychological snake oil. Henry Fairlie shares my pessimism:

> The curious thing about our self-absorption—curious only until one thinks about it—is that it seems to bring so little contentment. People have never been more agitated about themselves, wondering all the time whether they are "actualizing" themselves to the full. Their little efforts are called "self-improvement," but always a self-improvement, as it turns out, that is measured only by how good one feels about oneself. In bookstores there are sections that are devoted to "Sexuality and Self-improvement," and the placing of the two together tells how shallow is the exercise. People watch their moods and feelings now as they watch the bathroom scales and turn to new therapies in the same way as to new diets. But this search for self-pleasing brings no contentment. They are still agitated. There must be better. There must be more. This discontent is always one of the punishments of Pride, the consequence of the illusions of self-sufficiency that it encourages.[4]

Perhaps I am being too harsh. One might argue that pop psychology is justified by the transient boosts it provides, even if the boosts do not endure. This much, however, seems clear: the mood in all this is one of self-absorption. Happiness is sought by looking for it within yourself, not by losing yourself as you concentrate on others.

When self-indulgence is elevated to spiritual exercise, and self-fulfillment is the ultimate concern, we have made a religion of ourselves. Fidelity to oneself becomes the supreme ethic. As Wayne Dyer writes in *Your Erroneous Zones*, "Using yourself as a guide and not needing the approval of an outside force is the most religious experience you can have."[5] This is precisely the type of advice American Psychological Association president Donald Campbell had in mind when chastising psychologists for encouraging people to gratify themselves and to discard the moral wisdom of social evolution.[6]

By encouraging people to retreat from social obligation into their own inner space, the self-indulgent approach also covers over the reality of evil. Close your eyes, say "I'm OK, you're OK," and you may be able to escape noticing our deep-seated inclination to evil. But it's like putting Band-Aids on cancer. Fairlie makes the point with sharpened teeth:

> People are inventing gods for themselves, with what I have elsewhere called their Do-It-Yourself God Kits. But they are gods who do not demand much of them, and they certainly are not gods who punish, although they are allowed to reward. . . . Above all they are gods who will not trouble them with the fact of evil. The problems of evil, suffering and death are not confronted, but evaded and dismissed.[7]

COUNSELING AND PSYCHOTHERAPY

Most of us would probably agree that the pop psychology peddled to the mass consumer market delivers less than it promises. But what about direct person-to-person counseling?

To talk with a sensitive, caring person eyeball-to-eyeball is a different experience from passively reading a book or hearing an inspirational talk. Research has evaluated the effects of helping efforts and, although the results are sufficiently ambiguous to have provoked considerable controversy, we can draw some general conclusions.

Some of these research studies have examined the effects of programs that attempt to change people. As you read more and more of these reports you begin to note a familiar pattern: when you examine people's self-reports after some experience, the results are very encouraging—people say they have grown from it; when you examine how people actually behave in situations for which the program was preparing them, the results are often discouraging—people who have had the experience are not observably affected by it. Research on the T-group method of sensitivity training for managers indicates that the trainees afterward espouse a desire for openness and trust, but back on the job their behavior and effectiveness is rarely altered to any significant extent.[8] During the late 1960s several private companies conducted experiments in the education of disadvantaged children. Although begun with an initial flurry of heartening publicity over its apparent successes, the movement soon disappeared because the contractors were paid for test-score improvements and the improvements were not there.[9] Prisoner rehabilitation programs have often followed the same pattern: they begin with high hopes and end without measurable success.

Must we therefore discount the cherished conjectures of generations of would-be helpers? Granted, people are not easily changed. But perhaps more encouraging results would be obtained if we counseled people more comprehensively. Some years ago the Ford Foundation invested $450,000 in Project Phoenix, an experimental program that sought to motivate 240 eighth- and ninth-grade Phoenix, Arizona students to, among other things, do better in school. Most of these youths had a rugged past: they came from impoverished families, and they were not doing well in school. The children were paired with outstanding college students who throughout the school year counseled them, helped them with their studies, and provided an admired model of what they might become. But, alas, there was no discernible impact on the children's grades, test scores, or school attendance.[10]

An even more ambitious project, involving over 500 five- to thirteen-year-old boys, many of whom seemed bound for delinquency, was undertaken in urban areas of eastern Massachusetts during the early 1940s. By the flip of a coin, half of the boys were assigned to an intensive treatment program that, for five years, gave them twice-monthly home visits by counselors and, as the need arose, academic tutoring, medical attention, and assistance to their families. Most of the boys were also brought into contact with the Boy Scouts, the YMCA, or other community programs. By 1979, some thirty years after the end of the program, Joan McCord managed to locate 97% of the now grown participants and to assess the impact of the treatment by questionnaire and by check of public records from courts, mental hospitals, etc.[11]

Assessing the treatment program in the way most evaluations are conducted—by looking at those who participated— yielded encouraging results. Many of the men offered glowing testimonials. Some wrote that the activities kept them off the streets and out of trouble. Others noted that the program "helped me to have faith and trust in other people," that "I was put on the right road," and that it "helped prepare me for manhood." A few noted that had it not been for their counselors "I would probably be in jail," "My life would have gone the other way," or "I think I would have ended up in a life of crime." The court records offered apparent support for these testimonials. Even among the "difficult" boys in the program, 66% had developed no official juvenile crime record.

But did the program really do any good? Or did the testimonials and court data just create an illusion of its efficacy? The extraordinary feature of the "Cambridge-Somerville Youth Study," as this project is called, was that for every boy who participated there was a similar boy who did not participate. It turns out that of these untreated predelinquent boys, 70% developed no juvenile record. Moreover, many other objective comparisons also failed to find any positive effects of the treatment. In fact, on some measures, such as likelihood of a second crime, alcoholic tendencies, death rate, and job satisfaction, there appeared to be slight *negative* effects from the treatment. Perhaps, McCord speculated, the intervention created a dependency, or maybe it generated such high expectations that greater frustration was later experienced, or perhaps it led the boys to view themselves as requiring help.

Although the application of common-sense wisdom has seldom produced significant observed benefits, the record is not one of complete failure. Harrison McKay and colleagues approached what must be the maximum possible impact by giving 248 severely deprived and undernourished Colombian children a massive program combining nutritional, health, and educational treatments.[12] In the experimental groups, children under age seven participated in a preschool enrichment program six hours a day, five days a week for up to three and one-half years—more than 4,000 treatment hours. By the time they graduated from the program, the treated children had developed intellectual abilities far closer to upper-class children from their city than had untreated children. Moreover, the younger the children were when entering the treatment program, the greater were the benefits. And the intelligence gains were still evident after a year of elementary school.

The varying results of the Phoenix, Cambridge-Somerville, and Colombian studies typify the findings of other less ambitious projects. The picture is not entirely bleak, but neither does it encourage us to suppose that human problems are easily remedied by even massive doses of well-intentioned effort. Gerald Gordon and Edward Morse reviewed evaluations of social programs published in *Sociological Abstracts* between 1969 and 1973. When evaluators were affiliated with the organization, 58% of the reports indicated success. But when the evaluator was not associated with the program, only 14% reported success.[13]

If good intentions are not enough, then surely, we surmise, professional psychotherapy as practiced by highly trained clinical psychologists, psychiatrists, and social workers must have more to commend it. According to one estimate, nearly six million Americans a year find their way into psychotherapy, one and one-half million through the burgeoning Community Mental Health Centers. The American public now invests more than a billion dollars a year in psychotherapy.[14] Despite this enormous public confidence in the mental health professions, a spate of new books has raised a chorus of skepticism about their effectiveness (Martin Gross, *The Psychological Society*; Leo Rostin, *Passions and Prejudices*; Thomas Szasz, *The Myth of Psychotherapy*; Dorothy Tennov, *Psychotherapy: The Hazardous Cure*; Paul Vitz, *Psychology as Religion*). These critics assert that the pronouncements of society's new priests, wrapped in a veneer of science, elicit an intimidated acquiescence from lay people. Knowing they do not possess the solutions to life's perplexing problems, people are all too eager to put their faith in the "experts" who stand ready, for a handsome fee, to proclaim a methodology for living.

Gross speculates that one reason for the boom market in psychotherapy is that

> what the Psychological Society has done is to redefine *normality*. It has taken the painful reactions to the normal vicissitudes of life—despair, anger, frustration—and labeled them as maladjustments.

The semantic trick is in equating happiness and normality. By permitting this, we have given up our simple right to be both *normal* and *suffering* at the same time.[15]

The boys in my older son's sixth-grade class were a case in point. Most of them were sometimes lazy, unresponsive, or even a bit rebellious. No matter that this is how it is with many sixth-grade boys. Now such traits must be analyzed and interpreted. Most of them were therefore referred for psychological testing. One wonders whether such "psychologizing" does not create as many problems as it resolves, by provoking people to perceive life's normal downs as emotional catastrophes.

Why, at a time when college students are clamoring to become mental health practitioners, when Rosalyn Carter and the President's Commission on Mental Health are clamoring for increased funding for mental health services, and when millions of people are walking testimonials to the healing power of psychotherapy, is there persistent skepticism about whether mental health services are really an effective remedy? The reason, of course, is that subjective testimonials are subject to an "illusion of efficacy." The controversy broke open with Hans Eysenck's claim, some 25 years ago, that suffering people not undergoing therapy are as likely to improve as those who do. This is particularly true for certain types of problems, such as depression and anxiety, and for certain groups of people, especially young, attractive, articulate, intelligent people who are suffering a stressful episode.[16] Therapists who specialize in such cases can therefore enjoy an impressive "cure rate," certainly much higher than those who treat people from lower socioeconomic classes suffering from chronic ailments like drug addiction or schizophrenia. (It does not take much ingenuity to surmise which type of patient the therapists therefore prefer to treat.) Since educated people are more inclined to view problems in psychological ways and thus to appreciate the services which psychotherapists market, the self-selected clientele is mostly of the desirable sort. In short, the critics assert, public dollars spent for mental health mostly subsidize the educated and affluent classes for treatments which are of dubious value to relieve them of problems that are not genuine illnesses.

On the other side of this controversy are the mental health practitioners. As the number of helping professionals expands, so the vested interests for mental health funding grow. As happens whenever public money has helped create a new occupational class, several groups representing the providers of mental health services have formed to lobby for the protection and increase of their share of the federal pie. Since it is currently an open issue as to whether psychological services should be included under national health insurance, the dispute over the effectiveness of psychotherapy is becoming a genuine political issue.[17]

While dispassionate research on psychotherapy has not resolved the controversy, certain conclusions do seem justified. In fairness to clinicians, let us accept the evidence as exhaustively summarized by two defenders of the faith, Mary Lee Smith and Gene Glass.[18] By statistically integrating the results of 375 controlled evaluations of psychotherapy and counseling, Smith and Glass claim "convincing evidence of the efficacy of psychotherapy. On the average, the typical therapy client is better off than 75% of comparable untreated individuals." Given the inevitable variations in outcomes, one may surmise that some gifted therapists achieve results even better than this average.

The Smith and Glass report is not, however, unmitigated good news for psychotherapists.[19] First, the optimistic claim is more modest than first appears. While 75% of people in treatment may exceed the average untreated person on some outcome measure, so also do 50% of the untreated people themselves. The modest effect claimed for psychotherapy is visually portrayed by Smith and Glass:

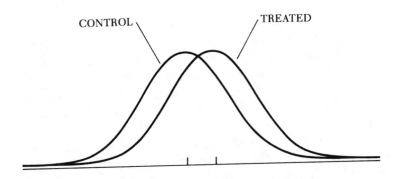

Figure 1.   Effect of therapy on any outcome.
(Data based on 375 studies; 833 data points.)

Moreover, all sorts of things that should occur if therapy is as effective as often claimed—more therapy sessions being better than less, trained therapists being more effective than untrained, therapy X being constantly superior to therapy Y—simply are not found. Distilling data across all 375 research reports, Smith and Glass found that it made no predictable difference how long a person was in therapy, who the therapist was, or what therapy was being practiced.

Some of the barely positive results could have been due to that familiar bias against publishing nonsignificant results, or to a "placebo" effect. We now know that before 1600, most medications were pharmacologically inert.[20] They were placebos—treatments which were effective solely because of the physician's and patient's faith in the medication's curative power. Physicians nevertheless maintained a prestigious position on the basis of cures associated with their placebo treatments. All therapies offer hope to demoralized people— the hope that accompanies a plausible explanation of one's problems and a ritual for surmounting them. Perhaps this is why different methods of therapy seem not to produce differing effects, for every therapy asks clients to have faith in its doctrines regarding psychic disturbance and its cure. If it is the faith, not the doctrine, that has healing power, then one would not expect one therapy to achieve results consistently superior to another. The healing power of faith probably also accounts for cures produced by native healers in primitive cultures.[21]

Especially since the advent of Community Mental Health programs, therapy for emotional disturbances is now widely available. Therefore, one might reasonably expect that such a surge in psychologizing would have a demonstrable impact on Americans' self-reported life satisfaction and on the frequency of mental disorder, just as modern medicine can point to its impact upon our society's death rates due to infectious diseases. It seems, however, that, except for effects of the modern tranquilizing drugs, the mental health movement has not obviously benefited our society, not even in places like Manhattan Island and Marin County, California, where psychological services abound.

Many new mental health programs assume that paraprofessional helpers are often as effective as professionally trained Ph.D.'s, suggesting that the professionals possess no special healing gifts. The assumption seems valid. Joseph Durlak summarized forty-two studies comparing the effectiveness of professional and paraprofessional helpers. The findings were "consistent and provocative. Paraprofessionals achieve clinical outcomes equal to or significantly better than those obtained by professionals."[22] Moreover, when one considers the mutually contradictory doctrines of various therapies, and the suicide and mental hospitalization rates of psychiatrists— most of whom underwent extensive psychotherapy during their training—it seems reasonable to conclude that the psychotherapeutic promise is overblown.[23] The exaggerated claims mostly originate with the enthusiastic supporters of psychotherapy—people such as advice columnist Ann

Landers—and not with the therapists themselves. Taking therapists off the "hook of divinity" may alleviate the disappointment that often follows inflated expectations of the curative powers of psychotherapy.

American psychology and American religion tend to view human problems as personal defects that can be usually remedied by prescriptions that are also personal: individual counseling or individualized faith. One wonders, though, whether pastors' involvements in extended counseling and therapy are a wise use of their time. I do not question pastoral care in times of crisis. Such care is a significant aspect of ministry. I am concerned with the tendency of some ministers to imitate unproven clinical methods. Pastors need not feel intimidated by the grab bag of mental health techniques, for the evidence shows that most psychotherapy has but modest effects. There is therefore no compelling reason for ministers to devalue their calling as preachers, priests, and shepherds. When the time spent in weekly counseling sessions with a half dozen church members preempts pastoral calling on the 200 other members who don't demand the minister's time, there has probably been a net reduction in the minister's effectiveness.

I am not contending that psychotherapy seldom does any good. Lack of dramatic positive results in studies of psychotherapy may indicate only that we have not adequately measured its effects. Just as a particular sermon can speak to a particular need, a skilled therapist can sometimes enable a person to work through a problem. Moreover, while any particular therapy is apparently not generally superior to another, certain therapies do seem more effective than others for specific problems, such as bedwetting, sexual difficulty, or a phobia.

If therapy has, on the average, modest positive effects—meaning sometimes it has a dramatic positive effect but also, quite often, no effect and even, occasionally, a negative effect—then there is sufficient justification for sometimes encouraging people to seek professional assistance. With a competent therapist one is more likely to be helped than hurt. Clinical psychology is a young and growing discipline, and so, perhaps, its place in the history of healing corresponds to that of medicine several centuries ago. As long as people are not encouraged to assume that psychotherapy possesses magical powers of healing, we can support clinicians in their struggle to help people cope with life's agonies.

But psychotherapy is, in fact, seldom viewed in this modestly positive light. Moreover, clinicians are no doubt subject to the same illusions as the rest of us. The available data from studies of clinical intuition and from research on psychotherapy confirm that therapists are indeed tempted toward overconfidence in the validity of their judgments and the effectiveness of their therapy. The self-serving bias, for example, may contaminate therapists' subjective assessments of their own results. In experimental studies, therapists have tended to take credit for good outcomes, but not for poor outcomes.[24] Hence, the clinician may surmise, "I helped Mr. X get better. But, despite my help, Mrs. Y got worse."

The principle of "regression toward the average" also contributes to the illusion of efficacy. Since people tend to seek help when things have hit bottom, any activity that is then undertaken may seem to be effective—to both the client and the therapist.[25] Therapy may also have a real, though temporary, calming effect by encouraging patients to ventilate pent-up emotion. This can make the therapy appear more effective than it is. This illusion of efficacy is the result neither of fraud nor insincerity, but rather of the difficulty we all suffer in discerning reality. Such illusory thinking is no more true of clinicians than the rest of us, but we should not exempt clinicians from the human condition. Doing so does us no good and is unfair to them. Again, my point is not to denigrate psychotherapy, but to place it in a perspective more helpful to us, more fair to the therapist.

If my comments seem unduly pessimistic then flip the coin and you will find a much happier side. I have not argued that people fail to improve with psychotherapy; they do improve! In fact, the news is even better than this—most of us do remarkably well at coping with life. By talking with our friends and in other ways struggling to climb out of life's pits, we usually surmount problems, at least for a while. Moreover, the sympathy and friendly counsel we offer our troubled friends often is virtually as helpful as the counsel offered by professional clinicians. Sadly, one without intimate friends, or without acquaintances willing to discuss one's problems, must sometimes turn to a surrogate friend, the therapist. Perhaps if we all felt less intimidated by the supposed healing powers of the professionals, we would be more willing to risk becoming involved with those who are troubled.

CHAPTER 11

Self-Serving Religion

The tendency to clutch at hopes for an easy road to health, wealth, and peace of mind occurs also in the church. There, a tension exists between religion focused on worship of God and religion focused on meeting our needs. Since God is "for us," worshiping him hardly violates our needs. However, when the worship of God recedes into the background and the satisfaction of our needs moves to the fore, various techniques for "manipulating God" begin to pervert religion into mere superstition. Such activity is not authenticated by being carried out in the name of Jesus and Christianity. Recall Jesus' caution that some who preach and cast out devils in his name will be told at the end of the world that he never knew them. Not everyone who says "Lord, Lord" is a part of the kingdom.

In our culture, superstitious religion is most obvious among certain groups on the fringe of Christianity. A recent mass mailing from the Don Stewart Evangelistic Association in Phoenix invited me to use a convenient clip-out form to check off my desired miracle. "Your letter is my Trigger of Faith," I am assured, triggering God to answer the prayer Stewart will offer in my behalf. All I need do is check off my need, be it "money to pay bills," "freedom from narcotics," "solution to family problems," or a "better car." Stewart's monthly *Miracle* newspaper publishes letters which explain how, after sending Stewart money, miracles have indeed happened. A typical letter writer explained that "The last time I sent $10 to you to be used for God's work, God blessed me with an unexpected check in the amount of $159.74. I just can't out-give God." (If giving is that great an investment scheme why not put the $159.74 back on Stewart?)

One of Stewart's mailings enclosed a "miracle prayer cloth" which had touched Stewart's body. Like the woman who was healed upon touching Jesus' garment, I, too, could unleash God's miraculous power for whatever need I felt if I would write a wish for myself and for a friend on the prayer-cloth envelope, put it under my pillow for the night, mail it to Stewart first thing the next morning, and then know that after three days and nights of ardent fasting and prayer by Stewart

> (that's how long Jesus was in the tomb before He was raised by a miracle) *THIS VERY SAME PIECE OF SHIRT MATERIAL from my body* will be sent back to you in the very envelope where you wrote your request. This is our point-of-release to expect something better from God. When you get this prayer cloth back, you are to carry it with you as a sign of our united faith for your SPECIAL MIRACLE.

Monetary offerings are, of course, also encouraged (with the reminder of Jesus' words, "Give and it shall be given").

I decided to test the Stewart miracle system: I asked this "man of the cloth" to get God "to stop Don Stewart from exploiting suffering people with his arrogant self-deification." A week later, right on schedule, my prayer cloth returned along with a letter (printed to appear handwritten) in which Stewart assured me that "For 3 days and 3 nights your special prayer requests and prayer cloth have been in my private prayer chamber and I've been praying. I've asked God to give you this special miracle you need to put His hand on your loved one. I really feel good about it! Victory is coming." I hope he is right, although I suspect it will indeed take a miracle.*

---

*I am sorry to report that the miracle has not yet occurred. Stewart's latest mailing, a computer-produced letter,

> is the most important personal confidential letter I have ever written to you. That's why I sent it to you personally . . . Kathy and I prayed and we felt led to tell YOU all about this. If I can't talk to you, then who could I tell about it?

Last night, in preparation for today's writing, I viewed Pat Robertson's 700 Club on the Christian Broadcasting Network. When I tuned in, Robertson was eliciting from God various cures, ranging from the sudden reconstruction of a polio-withered leg to relief of someone's nasal drip. Robertson also enjoys a hotline to God (via his "Prayer of Knowledge") by which God announces to him each one of these healings as they occur. "A woman's bad hip socket has just been healed," he proclaimed: "If you have a malformed hip socket, stand up. If the pain is gone, then it's *you*—God has done a great thing for you." (Implication: if the pain is still there, sit down—it's not you. God hasn't done anything for you. It must have been that woman in Peoria this time. But hang in there; God, like Santa Claus, may get to your house yet.) One commonalty that Robertson and other faith healers share with Joseph Smith, Mary Baker Eddy, Sun Myung Moon, and most founders of religious sects is the claim that each makes to having received special revelations from God not available to the rest of us mere mortals.[1]

One wonders about such faith healers—do they and their followers have longer than normal life expectancies? (If so, they should get a break on life insurance rates.) If St. Paul were here today might he say again, "To their zeal for God I can testify; but it is an ill-informed zeal"?[2] And does God really play favorites? Do some people really have a special "in" with him, or a privileged influence upon him? "The refused prayer of Christ in Gethsemane is answer enough to that," suggested C. S. Lewis.[3]

Perhaps there *is* a real power at work in faith healing—the

Stewart goes on to explain that God spoke to him, explaining what I am to do with my money. Funny thing, God said I was to give some of my money to Don Stewart, to send him $20, even if I must borrow it. And when this mass mailing produces its expected donations, it will, no doubt, be another victory for the Stewart miracle system.

sort of inner healing power drawn upon by modern holistic medicine. Norman Cousins's account of how he mobilized positive emotions such as laughter and the will to live as weapons against serious illness provides a striking example of the healing resources that lie within us all.[4] All who harness the psychic contribution to healing—whether doctors, clinicians, or faith healers—seem most successful with ailments amenable to psychic modification. Occasionally, miraculous instant alterations of physical structure are claimed, but they are generally of hidden, internal ailments, such as tumors, where the probability of misdiagnosis is higher. Those who proclaim the healing power of faith seldom claim external physical changes, like the replacement of an amputated limb. Obesity is probably the most widespread American malady, especially among the people to whom faith healers minister, but one stretches to recall any testimonies of how hands were laid on and 100 pounds of excess fat vanished.

Self-serving religion has become big business. For those of us who think ourselves too sophisticated for blatant superstition, Jesus the candyman also comes in more respectable packages. The bookracks at Christian bookstores are filled with re-psycholed paperbacks offering "The" Christian formula for how to get God to meet our needs for happy homes, robust sex, easy money, inner peace. The new mass circulation inspirational magazines offer the religious equivalent to the Do-It-Yourself kits of pop psychology. One can find all sorts of success formulas here, like a "Christian weight loss plan" which promises results far superior to those of pagan weight loss plans.

As Richard Bube has observed, "The world is so full of people needing love, comfort, reassurance, relief from loneliness, deliverance from despair, and healing for physical and spiritual illness, that any declaration of the availability of these blessings is certain to be popular."[5] Listen to the Sunday television preachers to whom people flock. The message of many of these inspirational pep talks is clear: like picking wild fruit, all you need do is pluck the benefits, cost free. What a deal! Not only will such faith bring no more suffering, but also an escape from any present suffering. After all, Jesus did promise that "all these things shall be added to you" (never mind that he prefaced this with "Seek ye first the kingdom," and "Take up the cross"). With this faith one can, like the singers on the Lawrence Welk show, smile forever. For things to go your way, all you need is faith. This, however, carries the cruel implication that if things do not go your way then something is wrong with your faith.

Does faith really produce such deliverance from problems? Dare we question whether there is in this movement something more than another placebo effect? Miracles *are* certainly possible; if the God in whom we believe exists, he can do anything he pleases. If the universe has been created and is sustained by a living God, such a being could surely give material success, serenity of mind, a cure for cancer, or even an instant 100-pound fat loss. The question here is not whether God can do these things. Rather, the question is whether God is a cosmic vending machine to which self-proclaimed Christians can drop in a "coin" and get a cure.

Religious thinking, being deductive, frequently goes un-checked by systematic observations of how people actually live and die. As such, it is vulnerable to illusions, like the illusion that our actions control events which are really beyond our control. Although faith benefits us by satisfying some deeply felt human needs, Job's experience nevertheless reminds us that the rain still falls on everyone. No matter how much faith we have, our mortality rate will always be 100%. As Reinhold Niebuhr wrote, "it is easy to be tempted to the illusion that the child of God will be accorded special protection from the capricious forces of the natural world or special immunity from the vindictive passions of angry men. Any such faith is bound to suffer disillusionment."[6] Some of the questions asked about Job can also be asked of each of us: Would we love God for naught? And is our devotion to God a response to who he is and what he has already done, or does it merely hinge upon what we can yet get him to do for us?

It is ironic that "pop Christianity" is a religion practically guaranteeing its followers what they want when the Bible itself depicts its people receiving so little success. Contrary to the claims of "perfectionist" or "holiness" Christianity, there is little evidence—either scientific or biblical—that self-proclaimed Christians are freed from sin or perfected in thought. In actuality, the "heroes of the faith" were seldom successful. They were backsliders, not backslappers. They experienced tribulation more than triumph. They grimaced more than they grinned. In the Old Testament one seldom finds a saint. Noah becomes a drunken fool, David commits murder out of lust for a woman, and the prophets are hardly well-adjusted and serene. Jacob broke nearly all the Ten Commandments: He cheated and stole; he was a blasphemous, polygamous, ungrateful scoundrel. Yet, God declared himself "the God of Jacob," renamed Jacob as "Israel," and made him father of the Jewish nation.

Likewise, looming figures of the New Testament are portrayed in all their frailty. Paul is ever afflicted and struggles constantly to resist doing that which he ought not to do. Listening to the disciples one hears no glamorous testimonies of "how I overcame anger, selfishness, and doubt." Although Judas is the most notorious, at one time or another each disciple becomes angry, selfish, or despairing. Peter loses his temper, is prejudiced against Gentiles, and denies Christ. After nearly three years with Jesus, Andrew will not conceive the possibility of a miracle with loaves and fish. Nathaniel, when skeptical that anything good could come out of Nazareth, reveals his pride and prejudice. Unless Jesus would "show us the Father," Philip refuses to believe that Jesus and God are one. James and John, the sons of

Zebedee, crave the highest positions of status in the kingdom for themselves. Thomas not only doubts Christ's resurrection, but is also skeptical of Jesus' promise to prepare a place in the Father's house. Simon the Zealot, Bartholomew, Matthew, and Jude cannot even stay awake during Jesus' agony before his betrayal. The Bible is remarkably straightforward—it harbors no illusions about the virtue of its own people. It has no need for illusion: its hope rests not in the power of human faith, but in the steadfast love of God.

Despite Scripture's repeated admonitions to count the cost of discipleship; to worship God because of who he is, regardless of benefits; and to serve God by serving others— we are constantly inclined to accumulate fame and fortune and to try to harness God for our own immediate purposes. We practice spiritual ventriloquism, putting our words into the mouth of God, and believing the voice we throw to be the very voice of the Lord. When we make our own words our absolute truth, when we presume that what we decide to do and to proclaim is identical to what God would will us to, then, said Karl Barth, we have made out of our religion an idol. We have, in our vanity, forgotten the gulf between the little world of our own finite minds and the absolute "otherness" of God.

Evangelist Rex Humbard recently announced to his followers that he was going to Brazil to save 500,000 souls at a cost of $500,000. "A $100 gift means 100 souls saved. A $50 gift means 50 souls; $25 means 25 souls; $10 means 10 souls."[7] (That beats evangelist Billy Sunday, who used to say, even before the modern inflationary times, that he converted people at "less than two dollars per soul.") One wonders whether people who are so absolutely sure that God is on their side proclaim such in order to avoid having him on their back. When the Israelites argued that God would never let Jerusalem fall, because "We have the temple," the prophet Jeremiah spoke God's word in taking them to task for their arrogance. Presuming God to be in our pocket is the beginning of idolatry.

To identify our purposes with God's reenacts original sin. Rather than guarding against this tendency, "pop Christianity" legitimizes it. What better way to authenticate our Christian doctrines and social ideologies than to presume them to be a part of God's own doctrine and ideology? Donald Bloesch has noted that these temptations to and of idolatrous religion are the very reasons why a major thrust of the Bible is directed "not so much against godlessness or secularity as against human religion whereby man seeks to be God or to control God for his own ends."[8] The religious dimension of human existence is, as Langdon Gilkey has written, "not only the ground of its only hope but the source of life's deepest perversion . . . This is why human religion is so ambiguous and has been the seat of history's greatest fanaticisms and cruelty as well as of its transcendent spiritual grandeur."[9] The exaggerated promises in the claims of popular religion and self-help recipes are the foundation stones of modern Towers of Babel.

Martin Luther once likened humanity to a drunkard who, after falling off his horse on the right, falls off it next time on the left. Those of us who believe American culture is falling off on the right in its current infatuation with popular armchair psychology, with the mental health professions, and with therapeutic religion are vulnerable to falling off on the left by dismissing them altogether—their wisdom along with their errors. Surely, however, the sages are right: those who seek comfort before truth will eventually find the greater despair if their illusion crumbles. Despair results from the lack of trust that demands God's promises be fulfilled *now*, on our terms, lest we shrivel in resigned hopelessness. If we build our hope on the rock of truth, we will have to search deeper for comfort, but, if we find it, we will ultimately know a more enduring peace. Give people only what they want to hear and you give them a lifeline that may snap under stress. Give people *truth* and you give them a lifeline that, while harder to hold, will endure life's perils. As C. F. D. Moule concluded:

> We can make a long list, from the Bible, of objects in which people from time to time reposed their hopes, only to find that all proved false . . . God is continually weaning us from our false hopes, in order to lead us instead to the one Hope, which is—himself.[10]

CHAPTER 12

Christian Hope

I have contended that recent psychological research illumi-
nates sources of human evil and suggests how illusory
thinking makes us gullible to false hopes. It's difficult to
disagree with Arnold Toynbee's assessment that science

> has not been able to do anything to cure man of his sinfulness and his
> sense of insecurity, or to avert the painfulness of failure and the dread
> of death. Above all, it has not helped him to break out of the prison of
> his inborn self-centeredness into communion or union with some
> reality that is greater, more important, more valuable, and more
> lasting than the individual himself.[1]

If self-help manuals, psychotherapy, and self-serving religion
are not ultimate answers, then where is the means to deal
with the evil and illusion of human existence?

The answer, I believe, lies in the biblical proclamation of
hope. Although the Bible continually reminds us of the fact of
human evil, it also constantly couples this bad news with
proclamations of good news. Some of its strong images of hope
come quickly to mind: the rainbow, the promised land, the
incarnation, the resurrection, the new Jerusalem. The past
record of God's faithfulness and mighty acts is proclaimed as
grounds for our hope for the future. Over and over we are told
not to despair. God is the ultimate power; he will speak the
last word.

Here the Bible parts company with those thinkers, both
ancient and modern, who also sense the evil and illusion of
human existence, but find no hope beyond them. The Greek
tragedies remind us that there is no life so happy and secure
that it cannot tomorrow be devastated by catastrophe. But the

tragedies offer only despair. Modern existentialist philosophers, such as Albert Camus and Jean-Paul Sartre, also have seen through our illusory comforts. But they, too, have discerned nothing on the other side—hence their message of despair, meaninglessness, and absurdity.

The Bible well recognizes that despair cannot sustain us. As Jesus said, "Man shall not live by bread alone." We need a reason to live, a purpose that can pull us through life, an ability to discern meaning in the midst of tragedy. The sustaining power of hope is widely recognized today. As noted earlier, all constructive psychotherapeutic relationships offer a sense of hope. Indeed every cultural ideology, from Marxism to the American Dream, offers its own version of hope. With hope, people achieve more, live longer when in dire circumstances, and are less vulnerable to physical and emotional infirmities. Hope is fundamental to human existence.

Any hope can be defined partly by what it is not. *Biblical hope is not wishful thinking.* It is utterly different from naive, bubble-headed optimism, an optimism often spawned by pride. Many there are who try to ignore the realities of evil and suffering—whether through faith in human goodness and rationality or in the belief that God will spare them heartache —only to taste bitter disappointment. With their idealism depleted, and with their illusions shattered, they become disheartened, even cynical. To paraphrase theologian Reinhold Niebuhr, naive optimists believe that, with additional effort and inspiration, they, or their nation, or their cultural group, or their church can ward off the evils by which all previous civilizations have been destroyed. Andrew Carnegie expressed this kind of unwarranted optimism when, in 1900, he forecast that in the twentieth century, "To kill a man will be considered as disgusting as we in this day consider it disgusting to eat one."

Biblical hope, by contrast, is conscious of the human

tendencies which, in this century, have led to the extermination of 200 million human lives. It is realistic enough to look human evil, illusion, and even death straight on. It acknowledges our inescapable limits. As Peter Berger has written, "The whole drama of biblical religion is one long effort to wipe away [the] tears over the anguish of human finitude—but the effort is not an easy one, and its fundamental presupposition is an acceptance of reality and a turning away from the illusions of false promises."[2]

That there are no quick and easy answers is known by those who have fallen into the pit of despair:

THE HEALERS

My father guessed at work.
He gave me things to do.
We strangled weeds from the flower bed.
Flung basketballs at the net
That hung like a limp kiss,
Washed the car, walked the dog.

My mother guessed at a mother's love.
She went back to tucking sheets
Around me as I lay awake in bed.
She pulled her fingers through my hair.
She turned away. She held me.

My good friend guessed at leaving town.
So we lugged gravel, grinding gears
Up and down the western Pennsylvania hills.
We'd raise the bed and listen
To the gravel rush into a silent pile.

My preacher guessed at God.
He knew my answer; spread my sin;
Prayed; asked me to pray;
Sprinkled oil on my head;
Pronounced me of this world.

My doctor guessed at shock.
Strapped me down.

Hooked electrodes to my head.
Baptized me with volts.

I guessed at empty space
And all the breath
That I could spill to fill it up.

Jack R. Ridl

Although biblical hope is not naively optimistic, neither is it pessimistic. Remarkably, people who, like St. Paul, often found themselves rejected, endangered, and in ill health held to this "something" that replaced fear, doubt, and insecurity with a persistent courage in adversity; they had the quiet confidence of one "knocked down, but not out." Although keenly conscious of evil and sometimes grief-stricken, they were not morose. They knew they would not be spared the shadow of death. Yet they took heart in the conviction that "Even if I go through the deepest darkness, I will not be afraid, Lord, for you are with me."

Biblical hope recognizes and emphasizes the futility of attempts at self-perfection. Lewis Smedes has suggested that the false god of self-perfection drives us mercilessly: "The humanistic goal becomes a demonic tyrant." Many books, preachers, and advocates of "you-can-do-it" psychology challenge us to become the assertive, sexy, affluent, powerful, or virtuous self of our dreams. But when, after all our efforts, the promise of abundant life is still not fulfilled, we become frustrated by our physical, emotional, and intellectual limitations, by our laziness, and by the ever-present threat that death will undo it all anyway. Warns Smedes, the call to self-perfection "is the essence of what St. Paul called the commandment that promises life but kills us in the end (Romans 7:10)."[3]

St. Paul, who expressed unquenchable hope even in dire circumstances, knew that the search for self-perfection never satisfies, always leaving a feeling of insecurity. Not only did he acknowledge the presence and power of evil and death, he came to view all attempts at self-justification "as refuse."[4] Still he was hopeful. What is the basis of this hope that acknowledges the brute facts of life?

Hope is found in the experience of grace. Our first step toward encountering the God of hope is to come to terms with our not-godness—with our vanity and illusions. Jesus' Sermon on the Mount hints at the paradoxical ways by which comfort, satisfaction, mercy, peace, happiness, and visions of God are discovered: "Happy are those who know they are spiritually poor; the Kingdom of heaven belongs to them!"[5] Finding abundant life apparently requires casting aside our vanity and becoming as unpretentious as a small child.

"Christian religion," said C. S. Lewis, "is, in the long run, a thing of unspeakable comfort. But it does not begin in comfort; it begins in [dismay], and it is no use at all trying to go on to that comfort without first going through that dismay."[6] In coming to realize that self-interest and illusion taint our thoughts and actions, we take the first step toward wholeness. The new insights gained from psychological research into vanity and illusion therefore have profoundly Christian implications, for they drive us back to the biblical view of our creatureliness and spiritual poverty, the very view which, in our pride, we are so prone to deny.

The whole point of the Christian gospel is that the evil that oppresses human lives is so significant that God willed to experience it with us and bear it for is. Christians believe that God visited this planet as a human being and sacrificed himself on our behalf, thereby demonstrating the completeness of his love for each of us. This supreme act of grace is proclaimed as the key to human liberation—liberation from the need to define our self-worth solely in terms of achievements, or prestige, or physical and material well-being. Of course, few of us can live by grace alone, fully escaping our dependence on the bread of social approval. Still, if now and then we can lift our heads and sense the sunlight, we may at least be able to keep things in perspective.

Recall Pinocchio, who, while pondering himself, flounders in confusion about his self-worth. Finally he turns to his maker Gepetto and in a pleading way says, "Pappa, I am not sure who I am. But if I'm all right with you, then I guess I'm all right with me." In the life and resurrection of Jesus Christ, our Maker assures us that we belong to him and that we are set right. Thus while I can never be worthy or wise enough, I can, with Martin Luther, "throw myself upon God's grace." This is what St. Paul did, and in the surrender of his pretensions he proclaimed victory: "I no longer have a righteousness of my own, the kind that is gained by obeying the Law. I now have the righteousness that is given through faith in Christ, the righteousness that comes from God and is based on faith."[7] God is the great "I AM WHO I AM." And he likes me.

This "forgiveness of sins," as the Bible calls it, means that when exhausted in our quest to be virtuous, we can come bask in the warmth of God's love. There is tremendous relief in confessing our vanity—in being known and accepted as we are. Having confessed the worst sin—playing God—and having been forgiven, we gain release, a feeling of being *given* what we were struggling to get: security and acceptance.[8] Having cut the pretensions and encountered divine grace, we feel *more* not less value as persons, for our self-acceptance no longer depends exclusively upon the magnitude of our own virtue, wisdom, and achievement. The feelings one has in this encounter with God are like those we enjoy in a relationship with someone who even after knowing our inmost thoughts accepts us unconditionally. This is the delicious experience we enjoy in a good marriage or an intimate friendship, where we no longer feel the need to justify and explain ourselves or to be on guard, where we are free to be spontaneous without fear of losing the other's esteem.

Social psychologist Jerald Jellison has catalogued hundreds of ways by which we try to justify ourselves. He laments that since experiences of unconditional acceptance are, however,

> so very rare, the only way we have to cope with our anxiety is to try to stay in the world's good graces—by being "good," giving honest justifications whenever possible, and fabricating excuses when necessary. These lies, the criticism of . . . others and the continual self-consciousness give rise to self-doubt and uncertainty about our own worth. It is painful, and it is a pain familiar to all of us.[9]

To escape the pain, we weave ourselves a web of illusion. "Life is a cabaret," full of cheap thrills which divert our attention from threats and insecurities. We build our careers, our reputations, our bank accounts, but still we agonize. Will we achieve our next vocational goal? Will inflation erode our assets? Will our children bring us honor or discredit? The harder we try and the more we possess, the more we worry. The seductive voice still whispers: "You can do it; you can be happy, secure, and peaceful, once your ambitions are realized."

This is not to say that our careers, families, and finances are themselves mere illusions. In biblical religion such "worldly" concerns are vehicles for serving God. Rather it is to say that those things that matter most to us cannot be bought, won, or achieved. To think they can is to live in illusion.[10]

The biblical response to all our attempts at self-inflation is therefore to sweep aside the web of illusion which they create. We don't need to *establish* our self-worth; we need to *accept* it. As Jesus said to those who were burdened with justifying themselves by adherence to laws, "Come to me, all who labor and are heavy laden, and I will give you rest."[11] When our lives are grounded in Christ our hope becomes not so much "I'm okay and you're okay," as "it's okay even though we're not okay." This is the hope St. Paul proclaimed to the church in Rome:

> I am convinced that there is nothing in death or life, in the realm of spirits or superhuman power, in the world as it is or the world as it shall be, in the forces of the universe, in heights or depths—nothing in all creation that can separate us from the love of God in Christ Jesus our Lord. [12]

Hope is found in community. This first pillar of biblical hope—the experience of grace—cannot be fully known by isolated individuals. In the creation story the Creator immediately declares our social character: "It is not good for the man to be alone." Trying to go it alone is sometimes a prideful attempt at self-sufficiency, denying our dependence on one another.

In contrast to the private, individualized style of much of American religion and culture, the biblical people had a strong corporate sense. In Old Testament culture, tribes and clans were the entities of existence. So strong was social identity that whole groups were sometimes punished for the wickedness of individual members. In the New Testament, St. Paul taught that Christians were to think of themselves as parts of a single body, Christ's body. As members of one body they were to be continually bearing one another's burdens. Jesus developed his ministry with a group of twelve, and alluded to the corporate dimension of salvation by promising to be present when two or three gathered together in his name.

The proclamation that "God loves you" becomes far more than a "warm fuzzy" when it is embodied and transmitted in the life of a community—as we listen to one another, care for one another, and accept one another. When we model our relationships with one another on God's grace, his grace becomes tangibly present. "Koinonia," the supportive fellowship that sometimes exists among Christ's followers, is the instrument through which we can know in human terms what forgiveness, and valuing of our individuality, means.

James Dittes has demonstrated some practical effects of the

human transmission of grace. In two experiments he tempo- rarily led some of his Yale University students to feel either accepted or unaccepted by their peers. He then gave them a fabricated parable in biblical idiom and asked them to interpret it. Although the parable was actually incoherent (no two people could agree on what it meant) some students— especially those who were not feeling accepted— unhesitatingly declared its meaning. The other students, who had "experienced grace," so to speak, were better able to accepts its ambiguity.[13]

Hope is also sustained as well as found in community. The ancient dictum "outside the church there is no salvation" captures a social psychological truth. It is tough to be a minority of one, to hold to one's Amish convictions while living in Los Angeles, or to maintain an identity as one of God's children while living apart from the strengthening power of fellowship with like-minded others. Many of the modern sects and cults realize this. The People's Temple Community and the Unification Church have capitalized on the power of the like-minded group by isolating their members from others. That they have abused the power of the group should not dissuade us from harnessing its power to transmit grace and to nurture our sense of hope. The mutual strengthening provided by small, interacting groups has been evident in many Christian groups, dating back to the early church. The apostles Peter and Paul, freed from jail, met with their fellow believers and then went out to proclaim their message with even greater boldness. Whether the religious group consists of born-again Christians or members of a Catholic religious order, the ardor and devoutness of the group often enhances that of its individual members.

Finally, it is precisely because human evil is collective, as well as personal, that we need to counter it collectively, as well as personally. Evil is not just the result of a few bad apples that need to be replaced with good ones. It also results from social and institutional forces—the heat, humidity, and disease that help make the whole barrel go bad. If we are really to embody grace and live not just for our own petty self-seeking illusions, we therefore need a social environment in which we can experience God's kingdom on earth, and from which we can counter collective evil.

Hope is thus found both in personal encounter with God, and in the recognition that his presence is made manifest in our lives together.

Hope is found in the resurrection of Christ. If Jesus Christ was raised from the dead, his resurrection is the most significant event in all history, for with it comes the hope that death is not the last word, that God can and will give new life to those whom he loves. Compared with this hope of a timeless life, our hopes for fame and fortune are indeed trivial. After all, even the miraculous healing of one terminally ill would be but a brief reprieve from the common fate that awaits us all. "Physical healing" is really just a nice way of saying "delaying death."

However, before we explore the implications of this resurrection hope for everyday life, let's consider two objections to it. Some readers are likely already wondering whether the resurrection hope is not just another illusory belief—an idea created to protect us from the pain of thinking about our eventual destruction.[14] Isn't the New Testament supposition that Jesus rose from death merely a false myth that his followers needed to believe in? We must remember, however, that generally we see things that don't exist only when we expect to. Since Jesus' followers did not expect his resurrection, their post-death observations of him could hardly be explained as a product of their expectations. They never understood his messianic mission and therefore were forlorn at his death. The women who came to the tomb did not come expecting a resurrected Christ. None to whom he appeared were expecting him to do so; some of them didn't even initially recognize him.[15] It is also hard to imagine that the disciples later concocted the resurrection story when they knew that pushing ahead with the Christian movement would subject them to severe persecution under Nero, the Roman Emperor.

However, if we are honest with ourselves, we must admit to feeling some uncertainty about the resurrection hope. No belief system which claims to answer life's most profound questions—What is the source and destiny of nature? Who am I? What ought I do? Where can I find hope?—can prove itself. It can, of course, be argued that biblical teaching is credible: it doesn't contradict the brute facts of life, and it is, as I've tried to suggest in this and a previous book, essentially consistent with the emerging scientific picture of human nature. Still we must be honest. We must grant that the resurrection hope is just that, a *hope*, not a certainty. That the resurrection is something that cannot be proven is precisely why faith—the "leap of faith," as Søren Kierkegaard aptly called it—is needed. Hope is seeing with the eyes of faith. The Bible demands our commitment in faith, not our intellectual certainty. Jesus called people simply to follow him in faith. Peter leaves his nets and commits himself. Not until later does he verbalize his conviction that "You are the Christ." Those who await certain proof for their religious beliefs before joining the action will spend life on the sidelines. We can say yes to skepticism—to critical scrutiny of competing truth claims—and still say yes to a thoughtful leap of faith. When we approach life intelligently we will always see more than one side to any issue. But this needn't inhibit our commitment. Sometimes, observed Albert Camus, we must make a 100% commitment to something about which we are 51% sure.

One might also object that the resurrection hope can make religion an opiate that enables people to tolerate injustice and suffering when they should be fighting to relieve it. Karl Marx's critique of popular religion, which is echoed by today's "theologians of liberation," is not unjustified. There *is* a religious view that says this world is rotten to the core, so let's sit back and wait for the eschaton.

Although hopeful anticipation often does inject cheer into the present, biblical Christianity does not just hunger for pie-in-the-sky-by-and-by. The resurrection hope affirms that *this* life of mine, *this* being, is worth preserving. Likewise, Jesus' resurrection affirms all that he stood for, including his compassionate love and his solidarity with the outcast. By affirming these qualities and by giving us a vision of the eternal realities of God's kingdom, the resurrection hope motivates and directs our involvement here and now. Christian hope is therefore both individual *and* social, other-worldly *and* this-worldly. The person who is set free from clinging to the illusory securities of this world is the one who can most fully love and serve the world following the example of Jesus. To paraphrase Carl Braaten, "those who catch a vision of the future kingdom are like advance explorers, dashing ahead, but then coming back to lead the way."[16] Thus Martin Luther King could declare, "I have a dream," an eschatological hope that explodes into this world, and Jurgen Moltmann can write that

> peace with God means conflict with the world, for the goad of the promised future stabs inexorably into the flesh of every unfulfilled present. If we had before our eyes only what we see, then we should cheerfully or reluctantly reconcile ourselves with things as they happen to be. That we do not reconcile ourselves, that there is no pleasant harmony between us and reality, is due to our unquenchable hope.[17]

The experience of grace facilitates our visionary involvement in the world. Langdon Gilkey writes that

If men are to forget themselves enough to share with each other, to be honest under pressure, and to be rational and moral enough to establish community, they must have some center of loyalty and devotion, some source of security and meaning, beyond their own welfare. . . . The ultimate concern of each man must raise him above his struggles with his neighbor instead of making these conflicts more bitter and intense. Given an ultimate security in God's eternal love, and an ultimate meaning to his own small life in God's eternal purposes, a man can forget his own welfare and for the first time look at his neighbor free from the gnawings of self-concern.[18]

Gilkey is expressing Jesus' counsel, recorded in all four gospels, that one finds the abundant life by losing one's life. Like a rainbow, comfort eludes us when we drive straight toward it. Jesus vividly lived out his own insight. In his own life and dying, he accepted temporary suffering in obedience to God and in love for humanity, and thus achieved his own perfect fulfillment—his communion with God. Jesus could do this, and in a small measure we can, too—by viewing life's problems and questions from the perspective of the future. So often our attention gets riveted on the self-concerns of the moment. Ephemeral irritations—waiting in line for gasoline, having the television go on the blink, spilling grease on one's favorite coat—take on momentous proportions. We become prisoners of the puny.

Finally, by unflinchingly calling evil by its name, the gospel prepares us to recognize and address evil in the world. Kierkegaard, Reinhold Niebuhr, William Stringfellow, and contemporary theologians of the third world such as Dom Helder Camara differ in many ways but have this much in common: all of them have been prophetic voices whose moral acuity has not been blurred by viewing the world through stained-glass glasses. Each had a deep and healthy appreciation of the reality of evil and its subtle manifestations. Each recognized that evil is corporate as well as personal, and must therefore be contested on both the corporate and personal levels. In God's kingdom both individuals and political and economic structures are judged in the light of God's love and justice.

Although the facts of evil and illusion are disturbing enough, death is the supreme threat. We dread our own extinction and being separated from those special few people with whom our lives have been deeply intertwined. No one disputes the truth alluded to in an old Isaac Watts hymn: "Time, like an ever-rolling stream bears all its sons away; they fly, forgotten, as a dream dies at the opening day." The highest achievements of my life and yours will likely soon be forgotten moments in a far-distant past. T. S. Eliot's J. Alfred Prufrock knew this:

> But though I have wept and fasted, wept and prayed,
> Though I have seen my head (grown slightly bald) brought in
>   upon a platter,
> I am no prophet—and here's no great matter;
> I have seen the moment of my greatness flicker,
> And I have seen the eternal Footman hold my coat, and
>   snicker,
> And in short, I was afraid.

Life is like riding on a fast train: on the horizon, longed-for events lull far off in the future. Then they suddenly arrive. But then whoosh, they become but part of a dim past. Our existence is a rapid succession of never returning moments. Throughout my teenage years and early twenties I lacked this sense of life's transience. I could hardly wait for my firstborn son to get on with growing up and for myself to arrive at "real life," full adult life. Now I am where I wanted to be, that firstborn son is fourteen, and his three-year-old sister is growing up far too fast. Watching my children grow up is like viewing a time-lapse film of unfolding flowers. I wish that I could periodically halt time and savor longer the pleasures of each day, lingering over each affectionate smile on Laurie's small face. But it is as futile as my trying to stop that racing train. Several friends have recently died, my parents are growing old, and precious memories from my past are slipping away. Another of time's eyeblinks and Laurie will be old enough to read these words, if not yet old enough to grasp the poignancy of the life cycle.

Here in Michigan it is winter. In our house we turn the heat down at night, prompting my wife, Carol, and me to sleep snuggled under the covers like a pair of gerbils. The secure affection of this intimate relationship provides delicious moments. But the deeper the feeling, the sadder the realization that we are growing older and that there will come a day when one of us will sleep alone, and then when we shall both be separated from our children by an unbridgeable gulf. Pondering these troubling thoughts, I am driven to the conviction that either there is a loving God who is behind it all or else life is indeed an absurdity as people on this infinitesimal planet "come and go talking of Michelangelo." Having reached the halfway point of my life expectancy, I am increasingly driven to see life in the eternal perspective and to find reassurance in a Being whose love and power is my only enduring hope in the face of my frailty. Because of Christ's resurrection, I can hope for grace, both now and in the eternal future. In Christ, there is always a tomorrow.

This is the hope that moved the grieving hymn writer Martin Rinkart to return from burying his wife and write "Now thank we all our God with heart and hands and voices." John of Patmos gave us a vision of this resurrection hope:

> I saw a new heaven and a new earth; for the first heaven and the first earth had passed away, and the sea was no more. And I saw the holy city, new Jerusalem coming down out of heaven from God, prepared as a bride adorned for her husband; and I heard a great voice from the throne saying, "Behold, the dwelling of God is with men. He will dwell with them and they shall be his people, and God himself will be with them; he will wipe away every tear from their eyes, and death

shall be no more, neither shall there be mourning nor crying nor pain any more, for the former things have passed away. And he who sat upon the throne said, "Behold, I make all things new."[19]

At the end of his *Chronicles of Narnia*, C. S. Lewis similarly envisions heaven as a place where creatures cannot feel deprived, depressed, or anxious, no matter how hard they try. There is no "adaptation-level phenomenon," for happiness is continually expanding. This is "the Great Story, which no one on earth has read: which goes on forever: in which every chapter is better than the one before."[20]

For those who share this vision of the future age, it has begun already. It has begun among those who have linked life and destiny with Jesus Christ. "The new has come," writes the Apostle Paul. And Jesus tells us "The kingdom of God is in the midst of you."[21] This vision of a world liberated from oppression and suffering is a vision which directs and gives hope to our work here on earth. As Reubem Alves put it, "Hope is hearing the melody of the future. Faith is to dance to it."[22]

Knowing our inflated self, experiencing grace and ultimate security, living with gratitude, humility, and courage—this is the Christian answer to a world filled with evil and illusion.

> Lord, I have given up my pride
>   and turned away from my arrogance.
> I am not concerned with great matters
>   or with subjects too difficult for me.
> Instead, I am content and at peace.
> As a child lies quietly in its mother's arms,
>   so my heart is quiet within me.
> Israel, trust in the Lord
>   now and forever![23]

The psalmist prays in humble trust. We must first learn, not this particular prayer, but instead a prayer for the humility and the trust the psalmist so graciously lives.

Notes

INTRODUCTION

1. *Interpreter's Dictionary of the Bible*, Vol. 4 (Nashville: Abingdon Press, 1962), p. 361.

2 Margaret W. Matlin and David J. Stang, *The Pollyanna Principle: Selectivity in Language, Memory, and Thought* (Cambridge, Mass.: Schenkman, 1978).

3. Reinhold Niebuhr, *Beyond Tragedy* (New York: Scribner's, 1937), p. 115.

CHAPTER 1

1. Donald T. Campbell, "The Conflict Between Social and Biological Evolution and the Concept of Original Sin," *Zygon* 10 (1975): 234–249.

2. This natural, evolutionary account of moral rules is no doubt causing some readers to squirm. It may help to remember that natural and spiritual understandings need not contradict one another. If God is free to act through the events of his creation, then nature and spirit need not be seen as separate realms. C. S. Lewis, though hardly enamored of naturalistic explanations, devoted the first section of *Mere Christianity* to contending that morality reflects a "Law of Nature," a universal standard dictating what humans ought and ought not to do. Lewis was referring to a law of our *moral* nature, not simply a fact described by science, and he went on to insist that there was "Something Behind" the wisdom of our moral nature. Yet his argument that universal moral norms exist (itemized in an appendix to his *Abolition of Man*) is consistent with the thesis that our species has evolved universal social norms which balance and restrain impulses given by biological evolution. Campbell simply proposes the technical means by which Lewis's "Law of Nature" might have been established.

3. David G. Myers and Thomas Ludwig, "Let's Cut the Poortalk," *Saturday Review*, October 28, 1978, pp. 24–25.

4. Campbell, *op. cit.*

5. Philip Brickman and Donald T. Campbell, "Hedonic Relativism and Planning the Good Society," in *Adaptation-Level Theory*, ed., M. H. Appley (New York: Academic Press, 1971), p. 287.

6. Philip Brickman, Dan Coates, and Ronnie J. Janoff-Bulman, "Lottery Winners and Accident Victims: Is Happiness Relative?" *Journal of Personality and Social Psychology* 36 (1978): 917–927.

7. Langdon Gilkey, *Shantung Compound* (New York: Harper & Row, 1966), p. 226.

8. Ephraim Yuchtman (Yaar), "Effects of Social-Psychological Factors on Subjective Economic Welfare," in *Economic Means for Human Needs*, ed., Burkhard Strumpel (Ann Arbor: Institute for Social Research, University of Michigan, 1976), pp. 107–129.

9. Charles L. Gruder, "Choice of Comparison Persons in Evaluating Oneself," in *Social Comparison Processes*, eds., Jerry M. Suls and Richard L. Miller (Washington: Hemisphere Publishing, 1977), pp. 21–42.

10. Mark 14:7.

11. The adaptation-level principle emphasizes the relativity of satisfaction. Does it therefore rationalize social apathy? After all, it might be said, why bother to change the status quo if all is relative? Note that this argument makes self-reported satisfaction the ultimate criterion for social planning, rather than justice in the distribution of wealth. But even if felt satisfaction *is* assumed to be the ultimate good, social apathy is not implied. While money can't buy happiness, it can purchase freedom from certain types of pain. Worldwide surveys indicate that, within any given country, people with little money feel less satisfied than do those with more money. (Their dissatisfaction is greatest for domains like income and education where objective comparison is easy. Satisfaction is much higher for domains like marriage and family life where objective comparison is difficult.) But people living in poorer countries are *not* consistently more unhappy than people in rich countries. The satisfaction that an Indian couple might feel if their children learn to read and write roughly corresponds to what an American couple might feel if their children obtain college degrees. If, however, the people in poorer countries are sensitized to higher living standards elsewhere, they may then come to feel less happy than their more affluent counterparts in other countries. These comparisons of people within and between countries indicate the need for greater equality in the distribution of wealth.

12. Brickman, Coates, and Janoff-Bulman, *op. cit.*; Paul Cameron, *The Life Cycle: Perspectives and Commentary* (Oceanside, N.Y.: Dabor, 1977).

CHAPTER 2

1. I take this example from Harvey A. Hornstein, *Cruelty and Kindness* (Englewood Cliffs, N. J.: Prentice-Hall, 1976), p. 16.

2. Colin Turnbull, *The Mountain People* (New York: Simon and Schuster, 1972).

3. Langdon Gilkey, *Shantung Compound* (New York: Harper & Row, 1966), p. 115.

4. Stanley Milgram, "Some Conditions of Obedience and Disobedience to Authority," *Human Relations* 18 (1965): 57–75.

5. P. G. Zimbardo, C. Haney, and W. C. Banks, "A Pirandellian Prison," *New York Times Magazine*, April 8, 1973, pp. 38–60.

6. Muzafer Sherif has described his experiments in numerous books and articles, the most accessible being "Experiments in Group Conflict," *Scientific American*, November, 1956, pp. 54–58.

7. Reinhold Niebuhr, *Moral Man and Immoral Society* (New York: Scribner's, 1932), p. xii.

8. David G. Myers, "Group Polarization," *Human Nature*, March 1979, pp. 34–39.

9. Irving L. Janis, *Victims of Groupthink* (Boston: Houghton Mifflin, 1972).

10. Philip G. Zimbardo, "The Human Choice: Individuation, Reason and Order Versus Deindividuation, Impulse and Chaos," in *Nebraska Symposium on Motivation*, 1969, eds., W. Arnold & D. Levin (Lincoln: Univ. of Nebraska Press, 1970), pp. 237–307.

11. For a more comprehensive review of how social structure and psychic process conspire to legitimate evil, see Nevitt Sanford and Craig Comstock, *Sanctions for Evil* (San Francisco: Jossey-Bass, 1971).

12. For a recent review of this literature see Gifford Weary Bradley, "Self-Serving Biases in the Attribution Process: A Reexamination of the Fact or Fiction Question," *Journal of Personality and Social Psychology* 36 (1978): 56–71.

13. One theory explains egocentric perceptions in terms of rational information processing. For example, because of their generally successful past histories, people may be primed to infer more personal control when they succeed than when they do not. A competing theory explains the phenomenon in terms of our desire to protect our self-esteem and to present ourselves favorably. Recent evidence tends to favor this motivational interpretation—people are shown to evade responsibility for their failures and to actively present themselves in egocentric ways. Bradley, *op. cit.*; B. R. Schlenker and R. S. Miller, "Egocentrism in Groups: Self-Serving Biases or Logical Information Processing?" *Journal of Personality and Social Psychology* 35 (1977): 755–764; M. L. Snyder, W. G. Stephan, and D. Rosenfeld, "Attributional Egotism," in *New Directions in Attribu-*

tion Research, Vol. 2, eds., J. H. Harvey, W. Ickes, and R. F. Kidd (Hillsdale, N. J.: Lawrence Erlbaum, 1978, pp. 91-117); Myron Zuckerman, "Attribution of Success and Failure Revisited, or: The Motivational Bias Is Alive and Well in Attribution Theory," *Journal of Personality* 47 (1979): 245–287.

14. See Dale T. Miller and Michael Ross, "Self-Serving Biases in the Attribution of Causality: Fact or Fiction?" *Psychological Bulletin* 82 (1975): 213–225.

15. Anthony Greenwald, "The Totalitarian Ego: Fabrication and Revision of Personal History," *Social Psychology Bulletin* No. 78–5, Ohio State University, 1978; Robert M. Arkin and Geoffrey M. Maruyama, "Attribution, Affect, and College Exam Performance," *Journal of Educational Psychology* 71 (1979): 85–93; Walter G. Stephan, et al., "Attributions for Achievement: Egotism vs. Expectancy Confirmation," *Social Psychology Quarterly* 42 (1979): 5–17; William M. Bernstein, Walter G. Stephan, Cookie Stephan, and Mark H. Davis, "Explaining Attributions for Achievement: A Path Analytic Approach," *Journal of Personality and Social Psychology* 10 (1979): 1810–1821.

16. Michael Ross and Fiore Sicoly, "Egocentric Biases in Availability and Attribution," *Journal of Personality and Social Psychology* 37 (1979): 322–336.

17. For details see Helmut Lamm and David G. Myers, "Group-Induced Polarization of Attitudes and Behavior," in *Advances in Experimental Social Psychology*, Vol. II, ed., L. Berkowitz (New York: Academic Press, 1978), pp. 145–195.

18. Laurie Larwood, "Swine Flu: A Field Study of Self-Serving Biases," *Journal of Applied Social Psychology* 8 (1978): 283–289; C. R. Snyder, "The 'Illusion' of Uniqueness," *Journal of Humanistic Psychology* 18 (1978): 33–41.

19. Jean-Paul Codol, "On the So-Called 'Superior Conformity of the Self' Behavior: Twenty Experimental Investigations," *European Journal of Social Psychology* 5 (1976): 457–501.

20. P. M. Lewinsohn, W. Mischel, W. Chaplin, and R. Barton, "Social Competence and Depression: The Role of Illusory Self-Perceptions?" *Journal of Abnormal Psychology*, in press. (The depressed people in this study were also less socially competent, which may also have contributed to their depression.)

21. Donald T. Campbell, "Response to Dyer," *American Psychologist* 33 (2978): 770–772.

22. Barry R. Schlenker, "Egocentric Perceptions in Cooperative

Groups: A Conceptualization and Research Review," Final Report, Office of Naval Research Grant NR#170–797, 1976.

23. "Why Do Consumers Fear Inflation?" interview with George Katona in *ISR Newsletter,* Spring, 1979, p. 6 (Institute for Social Research, University of Michigan).

24. Laurie Larwood and W. Whittaker, "Managerial Myopia: Self-Serving Biases in Organizational Planning," *Journal of Applied Psychology* 62 (1977): 194–198; J. B. Kidd and J. R. Morgan, "A Predictive Informations System for Management," *Operational Research Quarterly* 20 (1969): 149–170.

25. Philippians 2:3.

26. C. S. Lewis, *Mere Christianity* (New York: Macmillan, 1960), p. 99.

27. I summarized the evidence for this conclusion in Chapter 5 of *The Human Puzzle: Psychological Research and Christian Belief* (San Francisco: Harper & Row, 1978).

28. Anthony G. Greenwald and David L. Ronis, "Twenty Years of Cognitive Dissonance: Case Study of the Evolution of a Theory," *Psychological Review* 85 (1978): 53–57.

29. Ellen Tobey Klass, "Psychological Effects of Immoral Action," *Psychological Bulletin* 85 (1978): 756–771.

30. Robert N. Bellah, "Evil and the American Ethos," in Sanford and Comstock, *op. cit.*, p. 178.

31. J. J. Rousseau, *Social Contract* (cited by Reinhold Niebuhr. *The Nature and Destiny of Man,* Vol. 1, New York: Scribner's, 1964, p. 42).

32. Gilkey, *op. cit.*, p. 112.

33. Karl Menninger, *Whatever Became of Sin?* (New York: Hawthorn Books, 1973), p. 14.

34. Janis, *op. cit.*

35. C. S. Lewis, *op. cit.*, p. 95.

CHAPTER 3

1. Reinhold Niebuhr, *The Nature and Destiny of Man,* Vol. I (New York: Scribner's, 1964), p. 16.

2. Genesis 3:5.

3. Matthew 5:18, f.

4. Langdon Gilkey, *Shantung Compound* (New York: Harper & Row, 1966), pp. 232–233.

5. Psalm 19:12.

6. Reinhold Niebuhr, *Beyond Tragedy* (New York: Scribner's, 1937), pp. 102–103.

7. Henry Fairlie, *The Seven Deadly Sins Today* (New York: New Republic Books, 1978), p. 45.

8. This is discussed at length in William Stringfellow's *An Ethic for Christians and Other Aliens in a Strange Land* (Waco, Texas: Word, 1973) and in Mark Hatfield's *Between a Rock and a Hard Place* (Waco, Texas: Word, 1976).

9. Alvin Plantinga, "Makes God Responsible for Sin." Response to Richard Bube's "Original Sin as Natural Evil" in *Journal of the American Scientific Affiliation* 27 (1975): 178–179.

10. *Interpreter's Dictionary of the Bible,* Vol. 4 (Nashville: Abingdon Press, 1962), p. 364.

11. Gilkey, *op. cit.,* p. 116.

CHAPTER 4

1. C. S. Hall, "The Incredible Freud," *Contemporary Psychology* 23 (1978): 38–39.

2. The most frequent answer is $10. (People typically reason that when the man bought the horse back for $80, he lost the $10 made in the initial deal, putting him back to zero.) The man actually made $20, as this accounting indicates:

	BUYING PRICE: *(Money Paid Out)*	SELLING PRICE: *(Money Taken In)*
Deal #1	60	70
Deal #2	80	90
TOTAL	$140	$160 (PROFIT = $20).

If you missed that answer, and this still does not convince you, substitute "bricks" for "the same horse" in the second deal. Surely it makes no difference what item he bought and sold. If that is still not convincing, get out some play money, go through the transactions, and see how much they profit you.

3. Herbert A. Simon, *Models of Man: Social and Rational* (New York: Wiley, 1957), p. 198.

4. C. S. Lewis, *Mere Christianity* (New York: Macmillan, 1960), pp. 18–19.

5. See Richard E. Nisbett and Timothy D. Wilson, "Telling More Than

We Can Know: Verbal Reports on Mental Process," *Psychological Review* 84 (1977): 231–259.

6. Elisha Y. Babad, "Some Observations on Sadat's Visit," *APA Monitor*, February 1978, pp. 3, 19.

7. See Nisbett and Wilson, *op. cit.*, for a summary of this and many other experiments.

8. See Nisbett and Wilson, *op. cit.*

9. Eliot R. Smith and Frederick D. Miller, "Limits on Perception of Cognitive Process: A Reply to Nisbett and Wilson," *Psychological Review* 85 (1978): 355–362.

10. Ernest R. Hilgard, *Divided Consciousness: Multiple Controls in Human Thought and Action* (New York: Wiley, 1977).

11. For a more optimistic view of the usefulness of self-report data, see K. Anders Ericsson and Herbert A. Simon, "Retrospective Verbal Reports as Data," C.I.P. Working Paper No. 388, August 4, 1978, Carnegie-Mellon University.

12. Francis Bacon, *Novum Organum*, 34, 46.

13. Dennis L. Jennings and Lee D. Ross, "Covariation Detection: Theories Speak Louder Than Data," paper presented at the Western Psychological Association Convention, April 1978.

14. David Halberstam, *The Best and the Brightest* (New York: Random House, 1972), p. 562.

15. Lewis A. Coser, "The Visibility of Evil," *Journal of Social Issues* 25 (1969): 101–109.

16. I develop this point at greater length in Chapter 2 of *The Human Puzzle: Psychological Research and Christian Belief* (San Francisco: Harper & Row, 1978).

17. See *Science*, July 21, 1978, p. 235, and September 1, 1978, p. 774.

18. Jack B. Rogers, "Pagan Greek Logic Revisited," in *For Me to Live: Essays in Honor of James Leon Kelso*, ed., R. A. Coughenour (Cleveland: Dillon/Liederback, 1972), p. 105.

19. Karl Barth, *Church Dogmatics*, Vol. I/2, tr., G. T. Thompson and Harold Knight (Edinburgh: T. & T. Clark, 1956), p. 716.

20. Charles G. Lord, Lee Ross, and Mark Lepper, "Biased Assimilation and Attitude Polarization: The Effects of Prior Theories on Subsequently Considered Evidence," *Journal of Personality and Social Psychology* 37 (1979): 2098–2109.

21. Melvin L. Snyder and Arthur Frankel, "Observer Bias: A Stringent Test of Behavior Engulfing the Field," *Journal of Personality and Social Psychology* 34 (1976): 857–864.

22. Craig A. Anderson and Lee D. Ross, "The Survival of Theories in the Absence of Evidence," paper presented at the Western Psychological Association Convention, April 1978.

23. Harriet Shaklee and Baruch Fischhoff, "Limited Minds and Multiple Causes: Discounting in Multicausal Attributions," unpublished manuscript, University of Iowa, 1977.

24. Amos Tversky and Daniel Kahneman, "Causal Schemata in Judgments under Uncertainty," in *Progress in Social Psychology*, ed., M. Fishbein (Hillsdale, N. J.: Erlbaum, 1977).

25. Arthur I. Schulman, "Memory for Words Recently Classified," *Memory and Cognition* 2 (1974): 47–52; Fergus I. M. Craik and Endel Tulving, "Depth of Processing and the Retention of Words in Episodic Memory," *Journal of Experimental Psychology* 104 (1975): 268–294.

26. P. A. Lamal, "College Student Common Beliefs About Psychology," *Teaching of Psychology* 6 (1979): 155–158.

27. Reported in *Saturday Review*, April 1, 1978.

28. Elizabeth F. Loftus and John C. Palmer, "Reconstruction of Automobile Destruction: An Example of the Interaction Between Language and Memory," *Journal of Verbal Learning and Verbal Behavior* 13 (1973): 585–589.

29. Mark Snyder and Seymour W. Uranowitz, "Reconstructing the Past: Some Cognitive Consequences of Person Perception," *Journal of Personality and Social Psychology* 36 (1978): 941–950.

CHAPTER 5

1. See, for example, Paul Slovic and Baruch Fischhoff, "On the Psychology of Experimental Surprises," *Journal of Experimental Psychology: Human Perception and Performance* 3 (1977): 544–551, and Gordon Wood, "The Knew-It-All-Along Effect," *Journal of Experimental Psychology: Human Perception and Performance* 4 (1978): 345–353.

2. Baruch Fischhoff and Ruth Beyth, "'I Knew It Would Happen': Remembered Probabilities of Once-Future Things," *Organizational Behavior and Human Performance* 13 (1975): 1–16.

3. Baruch Fischhoff, "Perceived Informativeness of Facts," *Journal of Experimental Psychology: Human Perception and Performance* 3 (1977): 349–358.

4. Daniel Kahneman and Amos Tversky, "Intuitive Prediction: Biases and Corrective Procedures," *Management Science*, in press.

5. Baruch Fischhoff, Paul Slovic, and Sarah Lichtenstein, "Knowing with Certainty: The Appropriateness of Extreme Confidence," *Journal of*

Experimental Psychology: Human Perception and Performance 3 (1977): 552–564.

6. Hillel J. Einhorn and Robin M. Hogarth, "Confidence in Judgment: Persistence of the Illusion of Validity," *Psychology Review* 85 (1978): 395–416.

7. P. C. Wason, "On the Failure to Eliminate Hypotheses in a Conceptual Task," *Quarterly Journal of Experimental Psychology* 12 (1960): 129–140.

8. P. C. Wason and P. Johnson-Laird, *Psychology of Reasoning* (Cambridge, Mass.: Harvard University Press, 1972).

9. Paul Slovic, "From Shakespeare to Simon: Speculations—and Some Evidence—About Man's Ability to Process Information," *Oregon Research Institute Research Bulletin* 12 (1972), No. 2.

10. Chuck Ross, "Rejected," *New West*, February 12, 1979, pp. 39–43.

11. See Amos Tversky and Daniel Kahneman, "Causal Schemata in Judgments under Uncertainty," in *Progress in Social Psychology*, ed., M. Fishbein (Hillsdale, N. J.: Erlbaum, 1977).

12. Daniel Kahneman and Amos Tversky, "On the Psychology of Prediction," *Psychological Review* 80 (1973): 237–251.

13. Henry A. Zukier, "The Dilution Effect: Normative Prediction Strategy or Counternormative Similarity Judgment?" unpublished manuscript, New School for Social Research, 1980.

14. Ellen Langer, Arthur Blank, and Benzion Chanowitz, "The Mindlessness of Ostensibly Thoughtful Action: The Role of 'Placebic' Information in Interpersonal Interaction," *Journal of Personality and Social Psychology* 36 (1978): 635–642.

15. This and other experiments are summarized in Richard E. Nisbett, Eugene Borgida, Rick Crandall, and Harvey Reed, "Popular Induction: Information Is Not Necessarily Informative," in *Cognition and Social Behavior*, eds., J. S. Carroll and J. W. Payne (Hillsdale, N. J.: Erlbaum, 1976).

16. Quoted by Nisbett, et al., *ibid.*

17. Under some conditions, statistical information can be persuasive. See S. M. Kassin, "Consensus Information, Prediction, and Causal Attribution," *Journal of Personality and Social Psychology* 37 (1979): 1966–1981.

18. William Strunk and E. B. White, *The Elements of Style* (New York: Macmillan, 1979), p. 21.

19. Walter Kintsch and Elizabeth Bates, "Recognition Memory for Statements from a Classroom Lecture," *Journal of Experimental Psychology: Human Learning and Memory* 3 (1977): 150–159.

20. Francis Bacon, *Novum Organum*, 47.

CHAPTER 6

1. See pp. 164–175 of *The Human Puzzle: Psychological Research and Christian Belief* (San Francisco: Harper & Row, 1978).

2. B. F. Skinner, " 'Superstition' in the Pigeon," *Journal of Experimental Psychology* 38 (1948): 168–172.

3. George Gmelch, "Baseball Magic," *Human Nature*, August 1978, pp. 32–39.

4. W. C. Ward and H. M. Jenkins, "The Display of Information and the Judgment of Contingency," *Canadian Journal of Psychology* 19 (1965): 231–241.

5. Daniel Kahneman and Amos Tversky, "Subjective Probability: A Judgment of Representativeness," *Cognitive Psychology* 3 (1972): 430–454.

6. I refer here to chance in the mathematical descriptive sense. Whether anything, ultimately, is "pure chance" is quite another question.

7. Summarized in Ellen J. Langer, "The Psychology of Chance," *Journal for the Theory of Social Behavior* 7 (1977): 185–208.

8. Harold H. Kelley and Anthony J. Stahelski, "The Social Interaction Basis of Cooperators' and Competitors' Beliefs About Others," *Journal of Personality and Social Psychology* 16 (1970): 66–91.

9. Mark Snyder, Elizabeth D. Tanke, and Ellen Berscheid, "Social Perception and Interpersonal Behavior: On the Self-Fulfilling Nature of Social Stereotypes," *Journal of Personality and Social Psychology* 35 (1977): 656–666.

10. Mark Snyder and William B. Swann, Jr., "Behavioral Confirmation in Social Interaction: From Social Perception to Social Reality," *Journal of Experimental Social Psychology* 14 (1978): 148–162.

11. Lynn Hasher, David Goldstein, and Thomas Toppino, "Frequency and the Conference of Referential Validity," *Journal of Verbal Learning and Verbal Behavior* 16 (1977): 107–112.

12. Lee Ross, "The Intuitive Psychologist and His Shortcomings: Distortions in the Attribution Process," *Advances in Experimental Social Psychology*, Vol. 10, ed., L. Berkowitz (New York: Academic Press, 1977), pp. 174–220.

13. E. Tory Higgins and William S. Rholes, " 'Saying is Believing'; Effects of Message Modification on Memory and Liking for the Person Described," *Journal of Experimental Social Psychology* 14 (1978): 363–378.

14. Shelly E. Taylor and Susan T. Fiske, "Salience, Attention, and Attribution: Top of the Head Phenomena," *Advances in Experimental Social Psychology*, Vol. 11, ed., L. Berkowitz (New York: Academic Press, 1978), pp. 249–288.

15. Paul Slovic, "From Shakespeare to Simon: Speculations—and Some Evidence—About Man's Ability to Process Information," *Oregon Research Institute Research Bulletin* 12 (1972), No. 2.

16. Richard Nisbett and Lee Ross, *Human Inference: Strategies and Shortcomings* (Englewood Cliffs: Prentice Hall, 1980).

17. Psalms 19:12.

18. Although our rationality is often limited and biased, no social psychologist would contend that we are devoid of rationality. Melvin Manis has summarized some of the social psychological evidence of human rationality in "Cognitive Social Psychology," *Personality and Social Psychology Bulletin* 3 (1977): 550–566.

CHAPTER 7

1. Perhaps the reader is inclined to wonder whether, in fairness, I should not also relate illusory thinking to a domain where I am a believer rather than a skeptic. I have already attempted this in a discussion of "Superstition and Prayer" (*The Human Puzzle: Psychological Research and Christian Belief*, San Francisco: Harper & Row, 1978, chapters 7 and 8), and I do so further in Chapter 10 of this book. Having suggested how fallacious thinking could contaminate my own religious faith, it seems fair now to direct attention to some realms where I have much less at stake.

2. Cited by Persi Diaconis, "Statistical Problems in ESP Research," *Science* 201 (1978): 131–136 (quoted from H. H. Nininger, *Our Stone-Pelted Earth*, Boston: Houghton Mifflin, 1933).

3. Ernest Hilgard, *Divided Consciousness: Multiple Controls in Human Thought and Action* (New York: Wiley, 1977), p. 132.

4. Some of these are described in Barry Singer, "Course of Scientific Examinations of Paranormal Phenomena: Resources and Suggestions for Educational Approaches," *JSAS Catalog of Documents* 7 (1977): No. 1, 1 (ms. 1404).

5. Victor A. Benassi, Barry Singer, & Craig Reynolds, "Occult Belief: Seeing Is Believing," unpublished manuscript, California State University at Long Beach, 1979.

6. See, for example, James Randi, *Flim-Flam: The Truth About Unicorns, Parapsychology and Other Delusions* (New York: T. Y. Crowell, 1979); Melbourne Christopher, *ESP, Seers, and Psychics: What the Occult Really Is* (New York: T. Y. Crowell, 1970); Morris Goran, *Fact, Fraud and Fancy:* The Occult and Pseudosciences (Cranbury, N. J.: A. S. Barnes, 1979); David Marks and Richard Kammann, *The Psychology of the Psychic* (Buffalo: Prometheus, 1980); C. E. M. Hansel, *ESP and Parapsychology: A Critical Reevaluation* (Buffalo: Prometheus, 1980).

7. Martin Gardner, "A Skeptic's View of Parapsychology," *The Humanist*, November/December 1977, pp. 45–46.

8. Bruce D. Layton and Bill Turnbull, "Belief, Evaluation, and Performance on an ESP Task," *Journal of Experimental Social Psychology* 11 (1975): 166–179.

9. Anthony G. Greenwald, "Significance, Nonsignificance, and Interpretation of an ESP Experiment," *Journal of Experimental Social Psychology* 11 (1975): 180–191.

10. John Beloff, "Why Parapsychology Is Still on Trial," *Human Nature*, December 1978, pp. 68–74.

11. Diaconis, *op. cit.*

12. Anthony G. Greenwald, "Consequences of Prejudice Against the Null Hypothesis," *Psychological Bulletin* 82 (1975): 1–20.

13. *National Enquirer*, February 7, 1978, pp. 1, 37.

14. Fred Ayeroff and Robert P. Abelson, "ESP and ESB: Belief in Personal Success at Mental Telepathy," *Journal of Personality and Social Psychology* 34 (1976): 240–247.

15. See Myers, *op. cit.*, p. 175.

16. Vernon R. Padgett, "Astrology and Economic Threat," paper presented at the Western Psychological Association Convention, April 1978.

17. Martin Gardner, *Fads and Fallacies in the Name of Science* (New York: Dover, 1957), quoted by Hilgard, *op. cit.*

18. Seward Hiltner, "Sin: Theological and Psychological Perspectives," *CAPS Bulletin*, September 1977, pp. 1–5.

19. Charles Huttar, "The Outer Space Connection," *Church Herald*, April 30, 1976, pp. 24–25.

20. Paul Kurtz, "The Scientific Attitude vs. Antiscience and Pseudoscience," *The Humanist*, July/August 1976, pp. 27–31.

CHAPTER 8

1. Richard E. Nisbett and Nancy Bellows, "Verbal Reports About Causal Influences on Social Judgments: Private Access Versus Public Theories," *Journal of Personality and Social Psychology* 35 (1977): 613–624.

2. Evidence for this is summarized in Myers, *The Human Puzzle: Psychological Research and Christian Belief* (San Francisco: Harper & Row, 1978), pp. 243–255.

3. Lee Ross, "The Intuitive Psychologist and His Shortcomings: Distortions in the Attribution Process," *Advances in Experimental Social Psychology*, Vol. 10, ed., L. Berkowitz (New York: Academic Press, 1977), pp. 174–220.

4. Ulric Neisser, *Cognition and Reality: Principles and Implications of Cognitive Psychology* (San Francisco: Freeman, 1976), p. 80.

5. C. R. Snyder, "Why Horoscopes Are True: The Effects of Specificity on Acceptance of Astrological Interpretations," *Journal of Clinical Psychology* 30 (1974): 577–580.

6. Richard E. Petty and Timothy C. Brock, "Effects of 'Barnum' Personality Assessments on Cognitive Behavior," *Journal of Consulting and Clinical Psychology*, in press.

7. C. R. Snyder, Randee Jae Shenkel and Carol R. Lowery, "Acceptance of Personality Interpretations: The 'Barnum Effect' and Beyond," *Journal of Consulting and Clinical Psychology* 45 (1977): 104–114.

8. For a review of other evidence supporting this point see Barry R. Schlenker, "Egocentric Perceptions in Cooperative Groups: A Conceptualization and Research Review," Final Grant Report to the Organizational Effectiveness Research Programs, Office of Naval Research, Arlington, Virginia, 22217 (November 1, 1976).

9. D. H. Naftulin, J. E. Ware, Jr., and F. A. Donnelly, "The Doctor Fox Lecture: A Paradigm of Educational Seduction," *Journal of Medical Education* 48 (1973): 630–635.

10. Edmund Bourne, "Can We Describe an Individual's Personality? Agreement on Stereotype Versus Individual Attributes," *Journal of Personality and Social Psychology* 35 (1977): 863–872.

11. Paul E. Meehl, "Wanted—A Good Cookbook," *American Psychologist* 11 (1956): 262–272.

12. Loren J. Chapman and Jean P. Chapman, "Genesis of Popular but Erroneous Psychodiagnostic Observations," *Journal of Abnormal Psychology* 74 (1969): 271–280.

13. Ray Jeffery, "The Psychologist as an Expert Witness on the Issue of Insanity," *American Psychologist* 19 (1964): 838–843.

14. Zev W. Wanderer, "Validity of Clinical Judgments Based on Human Figure Drawings," *Journal of Consulting and Clinical Psychology* 33 (1969): 143–150.

15. Amos Tversky and Daniel Kahneman, "Availability: A Heuristic for Judging Frequency and Probability," *Cognitive Psychology* 5 (1973): 207–232.

16. David L. Rosenhan, "On Being Sane in Insane Places," *Science* 179 (1973): 250–258.

17. Robert Coles, "New Forms of the Sin of Pride," *New Review of Books and Religion*, December 1977, p. 3.

18. See, for example, Alexander Thomas and Stella Chess, *Temperament and Development* (New York: Brunner/Mazel, 1977), John C. Loehlin

and Robert C. Nichols, *Heredity, Environment, and Personality: A Study of 850 Sets of Twins* (Austin: University of Texas Press, 1976), and Constance Holden, "Identical Twins Reared Apart," *Science* 207 (1980) 1323–1325, 1327–1328.

19. For examples see Jerome Kagan, "The Parental Love Trap," *Psychology Today*, August 1978, pp. 54–66, 91.

20. Lee Ross, Mark R. Lepper, Fritz Strack, and Julia Steinmetz, "Social Explanation and Social Expectation: Effects of Real and Hypothetical Explanations on Subjective Likelihood," *Journal of Personality and Social Psychology* 35 (1977): 817–829.

21. Mark Snyder and William B. Swann, Jr., "Hypothesis-Testing Processes in Social Interaction," *Journal of Personality and Social Psychology* 36 (1978): 1202–1212.

22. Mark Snyder, "On the Nature of Social Knowledge," paper presented at the Midwestern Psychological Association Convention, 1978.

23. Lewis R. Goldberg, "Simple Models or Simple Processes? Some Research on Clinical Judgments," *American Psychologist* 23 (1968): 483–496.

24. Stuart Oskamp, "Overconfidence in Case-Study Judgments," *Journal of Consulting Psychology* 29 (1965): 261–265.

25. Paul E. Meehl's analysis in *Clinical vs. Statistical Prediction: A Theoretical Analysis and a Review of Evidence* (Minneapolis: University of Minnesota Press, 1954) has withstood subsequent scrutiny (e.g., Goldberg, *op. cit.*; Jack Sawyer, "Measurement *and* Prediction, Clinical *and* Statistical," *Psychological Bulletin* 66, 1966, 178–200).

26. Robyn M. Dawes, "Shallow Psychology," in *Cognition and Social Behavior*, eds., J. S. Carroll and J. W. Payne (Hillsdale, N. J.: Erlbaum, 1976), pp. 1–11.

27. *Ibid*, p. 7.

28. Goldberg, *op. cit.*

CHAPTER 9

1. I Cor. 1:20.

2. James Daane, "The Two Faces of Arminianism," *The Banner*, September 1, 1978, pp. 10–11.

3. Jack B. Rogers, "Pagan Greek Logic Revisited," in *For Me to Live: Essays in Honor of James Leon Kelso*, ed., R. A. Coughenour (Cleveland: Dillon/Liederback, 1972), pp. 107–108.

4. Anthony Bloom, *God and Man* (New York: Newman/Paulist, 1971), p. 36.

5. Lesslie Newbigin, as quoted by Gordon Allport, *The Nature of Prejudice* (Cambridge, Mass.: Addison-Wesley, 1954), p. 451.

6. Lewis Thomas, "Hubris in Science?" *Science* 200 (1978): 1459–1462.

7. Glenn Weaver, "Teaching Introductory Psychology from a Christian Perspective," unpublished manuscript, Calvin College, 1978.

8. Indeed, this book illustrates the interplay between experimentation and insights provided by various everyday examples. The experimental results "ring true," phenomenologically, and the phenomenological insights often suggest hypotheses for our experimental research.

9. Francis Bacon, *Novum Organum*, 37.

10. Frederick Buechner, *Wishful Thinking: A Theological ABC* (New York: Harper and Row, 1973), p. 20.

11. Norman Cousins, "The Taxpayers' Revolt: Act Two," *Saturday Review*, September 16, 1978, p. 56.

12. C. S. Lewis, *The Horse and His Boy* (New York: Collier Books, 1974), p. 193.

CHAPTER 10

1. George F. Will, "The Seven Deadly Sins," in syndicated newspapers, July 8, 1978.

2. Herbert Mitgang, "Behind the Best Sellers," *New York Times Book Review*, July 2, 1978, p. 20.

3. *Newsletter* of the Association for Humanistic Psychology, July 1978, p. 30.

4. Henry Fairlie, *The Seven Deadly Sins Today* (Washington, D. C.: New Republic Books, 1978), p. 52.

5. Wayne Dyer, *Your Erroneous Zones* (New York: Avon, 1976), p. 68.

6. Donald Campbell, "On the Conflicts Between Biological and Social Evolution and Between Psychology and Moral Tradition," *American Psychologist* 30 (1975): 1103–1126.

7. Fairlie, *op. cit.*, p. 15, 16.

8. See Martin M. Chemers and Fred E. Fiedler, "The Effectiveness of Leadership Training: A Reply to Argyris," *American Psychologist* 33 (1978): 391–392; and Ralph M. Stogdill, *Handbook of Leadership* (New York: Free Press, 1974).

9. David McClelland, "Managing Motivation to Expand Human Freedom," *American Psychologist* 33 (1978): 201–210.

10. *Ibid.*

11. Joan McCord, "A Thirty-Year Follow-Up of Treatment Effects," *American Psychologist* 33 (1978): 284–289; "Following Up on Cambridge-Somerville: Response to Paul Wortman," *American Psychologist* 34 (1979): 727.

12. Harrison McKay, Leonardo Sinisterra, Arlene McKay, Hernando

Gomez, and Pascuala Lloreda, "Improving Cognitive Ability in Chronically Deprived Children," *Science* 200 (1978): 270–278.

13. Gerald Gordon and Edward V. Morse, "Evaluation Research," in *Annual Review of Sociology*, Vol. 1, ed., A. Inkeles (Palo Alto, Calif.: Annual Reviews, Inc., 1975), pp. 339–361.

14. Estimate of Gerald L. Klerman, Administrator of the Alcohol, Drug Abuse, and Mental Health Administration, as reported in *Behavior Today*, October 8, 1979, p. 1.

15. Martin L. Gross, *The Psychological Society* (New York: Random House, 1978), p. 6.

16. For a review of literature on patient characteristics and therapy outcome, see Beverly Gomes-Schwartz, Suzanne W. Hadley, and Hans W. Strupp, "Individual Psychotherapy and Behavior Therapy," *Annual Review of Psychology*, 29 (1978): 435–471.

17. Even if mental health services have no healing power, they might still make economic sense—by reducing the enormous number of psychologically related visits to physicians.

18. Mary Lee Smith and Gene V Glass, "Meta-Analysis of Psychotherapy Outcome Studies," *American Psychologist* 32 (1977): 752–760.

19. For critique of Smith and Glass see Philip S. Gallo, Jr., "Meta-Analysis—A Mixed Meta-Phor?" *American Psychologist* 33 (1978): 515–517; H. J. Eysenck, "An Exercise in Mega-Silliness," *American Psychologist* 33 (1978): 517; Robert F. Strahan, "Six Ways of Looking at an Elephant," *American Psychologist* 33 (1978): 693.

20. K. Daniel O'Leary and Thomas Borkovec, "Conceptual, Methodological and Ethical Problems of Placebo Groups in Psychotherapy Research," *American Psychologist* 33 (1978): 821–830.

21. Jerome Frank, "The Medical Power of Faith," *Human Nature*, August 1978, pp. 40–47.

22. Joseph A. Durlak, "Comparative Effectiveness of Paraprofessional and Professional Helpers," *Psychological Bulletin* 86 (1979): 80–92. For a more recent example, in which professors and trained therapists were found equally effective in treating depressed and anxious students, see Hans W. Strupp and Suzanne W. Hadley, "Specific vs. Nonspecific Factors in Psychotherapy," *Archives of General Psychiatry* 36 (1979): 1125–1136.

23. *Wall Street Journal*, August 3, 1978, p. 1; Walter Freeman, "Psychiatrists Who Kill Themselves: A Study in Suicide," *American Journal of Psychiatry* 124 (1967): 846–847.

24. Gifford Weary Bradley, "Self-Serving Biases on the Attribution

Process: A Reexamination of the Fact or Fiction Question," *Journal of Personality and Social Psychology* 36 (1978): 56–71.

25. A 1978 Louis Harris survey of adult Americans found that four of five families seeking help for mental health problem believed the helping professional was "very or somewhat helpful" (*Behavior Today*, December 25, 1978, p. 3).

CHAPTER 11

1. One irony in all this is that some of the same people who offer to speak to God on my behalf (since I do not enjoy their hotline to God) object when Roman Catholics claim that the Pope may, once every eon or so, receive a direct revelation from God which he then announces *ex cathedra*.

2. Romans 10:2.

3. C. S. Lewis, *The World's Last Night* (New York: Harcourt, Brace, 1960), p. 10.

4. Norman Cousins, *Anatomy of an Illness* (New York: Norton, 1979).

5. Richard Bube, "Therapy Theology," *The Church Herald*, November 11, 1977, pp. 6–7.

6. Reinhold Niebuhr, *Beyond Tragedy* (New York: Scribner's, 1937), p. 97.

7. Rex Humbard, "Claiming a Country for God," *The Answer*, July 1978, pp. 1–5.

8. Donald Bloesch, *Essentials of Evangelical Theology*, Vol. 1 (San Francisco: Harper & Row, 1978), p. 98.

9. Langdon Gilkey, *Shantung Compound* (New York: Harper & Row, 1966), p. 233.

10. C. F. D. Moule, *The Meaning of Hope* (Philadelphia: Fortress Press, 1963), p. 9.

CHAPTER 12

1. Arnold Toynbee, *Surviving the Future* (New York: Oxford University Press, 1971), p. 46.

2. Peter Berger, "Gilgamesh on the Washington Shuttle," *Worldview*, November 1977, pp. 43–45.

3. Lewis B. Smedes, *Love Within Limits* (Grand Rapids: Eerdmans, 1978), p. 54.

4. Philippians 3:8.

5. Matthew 5:3.

6. C. S. Lewis, *Mere Christianity* (New York: Macmillan, 1960), p. 25.

7. Philippians 3:9.

8. Keith Miller, *The Becomers* (Waco, Texas: Word Books, 1973), p. 134.

9. Jerald Jellison, *I'm Sorry I Didn't Mean To and Other Lies We Love to Tell* (New York: Chatham Square Press, 1977), p. 155.

10. Thanks to Paul Fries, whose sermon inspired the preceding two paragraphs.

11. Matthew 11:28.

12. Romans 8:38–39.

13. James E. Dittes, "Justification by Faith and the Experimental Psychologist," *Religion in Life* 28 (1959): 567–76.

14. Just as I have suggested how belief in ESP may be explained by the mechanisms of illusory thinking, someone else might in turn offer a scientific explanation of my belief in the resurrection hope. Edward O. Wilson, for example, suggests that religion may be explained by the biological advantage which it confers: "We have come to the crucial stage in the history of biology when religion itself is subject to the explanations of the natural sciences. . . . Theology is not likely to survive as an independent intellectual discipline" (*On Human Nature*, Cambridge, Mass.: Harvard University Press, 1978, p. 192). Likewise, Harold Miller and Steven Faux have suggested that the religious belief in eternal rewards on the other side of death has the adaptive value of training people to delay immediate gratification in order that greater gratification can ultimately be obtained ("On the Commonalities Among Religious and Moral Codes: Proximate Analysis from a Sociobiological-Behavioristic Integration," paper presented at the American Psychological Association Convention, 1978).

Wilson's surmise that the explanation of religion destroys traditional religion neglects that the truth or falsity of a belief system is an entirely different issue from the explanation of that belief system. An explanation of your belief about the causes of inflation does not invalidate your belief. Following Wilson's logic, a satisfactory scientific explanation of atheism would undermine the intellectual credibility of atheism. I see no reason why a devout religious person need deny the adaptive wisdom of religious belief; indeed, I can more easily see reason to expect it.

Scientific advances undermine the credibility of popular beliefs only when they directly disconfirm the truth claims of those beliefs. This, I believe, *has* happened regarding belief in ESP, but not with regard to the truth claims of Christian faith (see Donald M. MacKay's *Science, Chance and Providence*, New York: Oxford University Press, 1978).

15. John Macquarrie, *Christian Hope* (New York: Seabury Press, 1978), pp. 173–174.

16. Carl E. Braaten, "The Significance of the Future: An Eschatological Perspective," in *Hope and the Future of Man*, ed., Ewart H. Cousins (Philadelphia: Fortress Press, 1972), pp. 44, 50–51.

17. Jurgen Moltmann, *Theology of Hope* (New York: Harper & Row, 1967), p. 21.

18. Langdon Gilkey, *Shantung Compound* (New York: Harper & Row, 1966), p. 234.

19. Revelation 21:1–5.

20. C. S. Lewis, *The Last Battle* (New York: Collier Books, 1974), p. 184.

21. II Corinthians 5:17; Luke 17:21.

22. Reubem Alves, *Tomorrow's Child: Imagination, Creativity, and the Rebirth of Culture* (New York: Harper & Row, 1972), p. 195. Cited by Bruce C. Birch and Larry L. Rasmussen, *The Predicament of the Prosperous* (Philadelphia: Westminster, 1978), p. 145.

23. Psalm 131.

Index